A Time of War
A Time of Peace

A TIME
OF WAR
A TIME
OF
PEACE

by
George McGovern
UNITED STATES SENATOR

RANDOM HOUSE
New York

*. . . For Ann and Wilbur . . . Sue and Jim . . .
Terry, Steve, and Mary . . . and for the late
Robert Kennedy—a great and good man
who fought and died to give them "a newer
world"*

Table of Contents

Introduction

There is some doubt about whether United States senators should be writing books at all. Our days are so crowded with diverse activities, concerns, and responsibilities that there is little time left for the kind of contemplation and painstaking care that ought to go into the preparation of a book.

There is the additional hazard that in this fast-changing world, one's views may be overtaken by events before the printer's ink has dried. Senators must make judgments constantly on complicated issues—judgments that are frequently based on all-too-sparse evidence and information. What seems like a sound evaluation one day may need to be modified as new insights, new information, and new developments broaden or inform one's view. Thus, it is politically safer to avoid the written word, or even the spoken word.

But encouraged by Robert Bernstein and John J. Simon of Random House, I have decided not only to put my views in writing, but to incorporate several of my speeches delivered on the Senate floor and elsewhere, beginning with my first year in the Senate: 1963. For the most part, these speeches appear in this volume as they were given at the time of delivery—except that I have written a brief introductory or concluding note to each of them in an effort to place it in perspective.

The chapter, "Foreign Policy and the Crisis Mentality," originally appeared as an article that inaugurated a new feature in *The Atlantic*, January 1967. The two chapters on the antiballistic missile and the draft were written especially for this volume, and the chapter on the Negro revolution carries a new section to update it in the light of recent events.

In a sense, this book represents an account of a first-term senator's efforts to find his way through the sometimes bewildering but always fascinating issues of war and peace, foreign policy and national security. Two earlier volumes, *War Against Want: America's Food for Peace Program*, published in 1964, and *Agricultural Thought in the Twentieth Century*, published in 1967, represents interests and efforts of mine in other areas of special concern to me as a senator from South Dakota and as a citizen of the world.

I can only hope that any reader of this volume will bring to it the kind of tolerance and generosity of spirit that I have been so fortunate to enjoy on the part of my constituents in South Dakota these past six years. Their understanding and counsel have given me both the courage and the desire to put my thoughts in writing.

George McGovern
U.S. Senator from South Dakota
July 1968, Washington, D.C.

Acknowledgments

In the preparation of the speeches, articles, and additional chapters which comprise this book, I am indebted to many people, including an able staff. My research assistant, Robert Sherman, gave special assistance with the chapters on the antiballistic missile, the draft, and the Negro revolution, while my secretary, Patricia Donovan, provided the expert editing and typing of the manuscript that she brings to all her work.

I am grateful to Richard Goodwin for help with the chapter on patriotism, and to Robert Eisner and Mark Pauly of Northwestern University for assistance with the chapter on the draft. Seymour Melman provided invaluable help with the economic conversion proposal and my views on reversing the arms race. Charles Phillips gave special help with the chapter on the American Negro.

Arthur Schlesinger, Jr., Fred Warner Neal, and Phyllis Piotrow read parts of the manuscript and made helpful suggestions.

I am indebted, too, to able and eloquent colleagues in the Senate who have inspired me—especially in the Vietnam debate where central roles were played by Wayne Morse, Ernest Gruening, Frank Church, Gaylord Nelson, William Fulbright, Mike Mansfield, Robert and Edward Kennedy, Vance Hartke, Albert Gore, Claiborne Pell, George Aiken, John Sherman Cooper, Thruston Morton, and Mark Hatfield. My colleagues Eugene McCarthy and Robert Kennedy later placed all of us in their special debt by making a direct political challenge to our Vietnam policy in their presidential candidacies. I am also indebted to Senator Gale McGee, with whom I engaged in a series of debates and whom I regard as the Senate's most articulate defender of Administration policy.

Cicely Nichols greatly improved the entire manuscript by thoughtful, imaginative editing.

I am, as always, grateful for the amazing understanding and patience of my wife, Eleanor.

Finally, I am deeply indebted to my fellow South Dakotans for the privilege of representing them in the nation's capital and for their generosity of mind and spirit in permitting me to speak out on the hard issues even when they did not fully agree with my views.

To every thing there is a season, and a time to every purpose under the heaven:

A time to be born, and a time to die; a time to plant, and a time to pluck up that which is planted;

A time to kill, and a time to heal; a time to break down, and a time to build up;

A time to weep, and a time to laugh; a time to mourn, and a time to dance;

A time to cast away stones, and a time to gather stones together; a time to embrace, and a time to refrain from embracing;

A time to get, and a time to lose; a time to keep, and a time to cast away;

A time to rend, and a time to sew; a time to keep silence, and a time to speak;

A time to love, and a time to hate; a time of war, and a time of peace.

—ECCLESIASTES, 3:1–8

PART I

American
Security
in Perspective

■ *The year I began my service in the United States Senate, 1963, was a year characterized by a cautiously rising hope for more peaceful relations between the United States and Russia. In the previous October, Washington and Moscow had stood in a sobering confrontation over the attempt by Soviet Premier Nikita Khrushchev to install nuclear missiles in Cuba—ninety miles off the Florida coast. Through skillful but potentially catastrophic diplomacy and naval deployment, President John Kennedy persuaded Khrushchev to withdraw the missiles in return for assurances that the United States would not invade Cuba.*

In effect, the two great powers looked into the graveyard of nuclear annihilation and backed away with a new appreciation of the need for peaceful accommodation. As Admiral Hyman Rickover put it: "The cold war turned a corner in October, 1962, and it has never been the same since."

On June 10, 1963, at the commencement ceremonies at American University, President Kennedy sought to underscore the growing need for a Soviet–American détente with a magnanimous plea for peace, which I regard as his greatest speech. Calling upon his fellow Americans to "help make the world safe for diversity," he said that "every thoughtful citizen who despairs of war and wishes to bring peace should begin by looking inward, by examining his own attitude toward the possibilities of peace, toward the Soviet Union, toward the course of the cold war, and toward freedom and peace here at home." The President concluded by announcing that the United States was stopping the atmospheric testing of nuclear weapons and would not resume testing unless other powers did so.

It was this wise, imaginative address that set the stage for the successful test ban agreement negotiated in Moscow and ratified by the United States and most other countries. Other steps were taken in 1963 to improve Soviet–American relations, including the establishment that summer of a "hot line" communications tie between the White House and the Kremlin. Also, President Kennedy offered in October to exchange American wheat for Russian gold as "one more hopeful sign that a more peaceful world is both possible and beneficial to us all." Unfortunately, after modest initial wheat sales, this mutually helpful arrangement was severely curtailed by American shipping restrictions, aggravated by the refusal of some maritime unions to load wheat bound for Russia.

I had long believed that the prospects for better Soviet–American relations could be strengthened by positive steps on our part designed to induce a more reasonable Soviet response. It was also my growing conviction that we could improve the chances for peace, enhance our international leadership, and strengthen our own society by reducing the enormous allocation of resources devoted to military hardware.

For more than two decades military appropriations had sailed through the Congress virtually without floor debate or discussion. Indeed, Congress would frequently force more appropriations on the Defense Department than the department had requested. Modest requests for funds to further education, health, or conservation would be carefully scrutinized, debated and discussed for days, and then finally passed in reduced form or rejected on a close vote. But funds for military use that came to many billions of dollars would be approved unanimously in a few minutes' time.

Believing that national priorities were not properly evaluated in this process, I took the Senate floor on August 2, 1963, to call for new and broader criteria of American security and national strength. Proposing a reduction of $5 billion in a military budget of $53.6 billion, I suggested that we were wasting funds on "over-kill" that were urgently needed in other areas of our national life.

New Perspectives on American Security

Eighteen years ago, as the pilot of an American B-24 bomber I completed the last of my thirty-five missions in the European theatre of World War Two. A few days after the completion of that tour of duty the war in Europe ended.

Our crew climbed into a battle-scarred bomber to return to the United States with the grim knowledge that we had used the most devastating weapons in the long history of warfare. Our four-engine bomber had day after day dumped explosives with a force equivalent to five tons of TNT on its targets below.

But we had scarcely reached home before news stories told of a fantastic new bomb that had incinerated 100,000 Japanese men, women, and children in a single searing flash. Suddenly, our five-ton monster lost its significance in the shadow of that 20,000-ton destroyer of Hiroshima.

Although the new dimensions of death were beyond comprehension, book titles in the afterglow of Hiroshima—*One World or None, Modern Man Is Obsolete, Five Minutes to Midnight*—attempted to assess the meaning of the nuclear age. Recognizing that humanity stood in deadly peril, we drew comfort only in the conviction that the new techniques of destruction were so terrifying that man surely would never again use them—would he?

Five years later, the A-bomb of Hiroshima passed into obsolescence, not because it was too fearful to use, but because it had been replaced by the H-bomb—a thousand times more powerful. Meanwhile, the Soviet Union became a nu-

Speech in the United States Senate, August 2, 1963.

clear power, and in 1957 Sputnik I ushered in the space age. Today, the two super-powers, America and Russia, have piled up nuclear weapons with an explosive power of 60 billion tons of TNT—enough to put a twenty-ton bomb at the head of every human being on the planet.

A single warhead from the American or Russian stockpile exploded over a great city would instantly transform it into a raging fireball 3 miles in diameter with a direct heat and blast capable of burning human flesh and collapsing buildings 25 miles from its center. Above a smoking crater a mile wide and several blocks deep, a gigantic, poisonous, radioactive cloud would rise 20 or 25 miles to rain down torturous death on millions of human beings not fortunate enough to be incinerated quickly in the initial firestorm.

In spite of this grim prospect, the accumulation of more and more devastating weapons continues. The great powers are spending over $100 billion yearly on arms—each side justifying its investment in the name of "defense." Yet, modern science supports the ancient biblical wisdom, "there is no place to hide."

Speaking to the United Nations Assembly in 1961, President John Kennedy said: "Today, every inhabitant of this planet must contemplate the day when it may no longer be habitable. Every man, woman, and child lives under a nuclear sword of Damocles, hanging by the slenderest of threads, capable of being cut at any moment by accident, miscalculation, or madness. The weapons of war must be abolished before they abolish us . . . The risks inherent in disarmament pale in comparison to the risks inherent in an unlimited arms race."

We accepted the logic of Mr. Kennedy's words, just as we accepted the earlier warning of former President Eisenhower: "There is no longer any alternative to peace." Why, then, does the arms race wtih its mounting military budgets continue?

Doubtless, a major factor is the uncertain quest for security through superior military strength. The Congress and the nation have willingly responded to the architects of our military security and have granted them unprecedented sums to insure the defense of our shores. Americans have felt that the growing technical complexity of the military art has required leaving the main judgments about security to our military officers.

As a freshman in the House of Representatives in 1957, I was tempted to raise some questions about what seemed to me to be a staggering military appropriations bill. But I lapsed into silence when an older colleague took the floor to say: "If our military leaders are wrong and we listen to their advice, it will cost us some money. But if these experts are right, and we do not heed their requests, it may cost us our country."

If that indeed were the choice, it would be dangerous to challenge the demand for more military spending. Every patriotic citizen desires that his country be prepared to defend itself against attack. Even the most ardent economizers—men who vote with zeal to cut funds for education, conservation, and health—are quick to shout Aye for more billions for arms.

I share the conviction that America ought to have a defense force that is second to none. But has the time not come to question the assumption that we are adding to defense and security by adding more and more to the nuclear stockpile? I suggest that we need to examine carefully the assumptions on which our military budget rests.

Have we remembered that the defense of a great nation depends not only upon the quality of its arms, but also on the quality of its economic, political, and moral fabric?

Is the size of our military budget the chief criterion of effective international leadership and national strength in today's world?

What is the mounting arms race doing to our freedom and the quality of our lives?

And most important of all, are we following a blueprint for peace or racing toward annihilation?

For the fiscal year 1964, we are asked to approve a Department of Defense budget of $53.6 billion, plus additional billions for the Atomic Energy Commission and the space program. That is well over half of our entire federal budget. It is greater than the combined costs of all the social and economic programs of the New Deal period from 1933 through 1940. A federal budget is, after all, a careful listing of the public priorities and goals of the nation. When we devote more than half of that entire budget to one purpose, we certainly need to be reasonably sure of our ground.

Current Defense Assumptions

To place these questions in better perspective, I would like to sketch some of the considerations that seem pertinent to our defense policy decisions.

Those who advocate surrender or passive submission to aggression, whether communist, fascist, or of whatever ideology, will find little or no support in the United States. Most of us are willing to risk death rather than give the world over to the tyranny of unchallenged aggression.

Likewise, few, if any, Americans would support the concept of an all-out military onslaught initiated by ourselves to wipe out those who hold to opposing ideologies. This, in another equally fundamental sense, would be a surrender of our values and traditions.

As a nation we have rejected both the concept of aggressive war and passive surrender. We have operated from the premise that the Russian threat is checked only because of our awesome military machine. This is the theory of "deterrence" that has guided our thinking for most of the period since World War Two. When one looks for a more specific answer to how that policy would be applied in the form of military strategy, he encounters some rather confusing and conflicting assumptions.

It has generally been believed that the deterrent or retaliatory power of America's strategic air power was targeted on the great cities of Russia, set to be used in the event of a major Soviet attack.

On June 16, 1962, however, Defense Secretary McNamara, one of the ablest men to come into government in recent years, made an important speech at Ann Arbor, Michigan. In this address Mr. McNamara spelled out the "controlled counterforce" or "no-cities" doctrine. The Ann Arbor speech set forth the theory that instead of seeking first the mass destruction of the Russian populace, we would aim our missiles and bombers at Soviet nuclear weapons in an effort to cripple their capacity to hit the United States. Only if the Soviets attacked our cities would we strike at theirs.

This speech touched off a wide-ranging controversy, partly because its success would seem to depend upon the United States' launching a first strike against the Soviet Union.

If the United States were aiming at the effective destruction of Russia's nuclear forces, how could we apply such a strategy unless we knocked out the Soviet missiles before they were launched from their silos? What military objective could we achieve by knocking out empty missile launchers after their rockets had hit American targets?

Secretary McNamara flatly denied that the United States has any intention of launching a first strike, but the "no cities" or "controlled counterforce" theory seems a most unlikely and impractical strategy. In lengthy testimony before the House Armed Service Committee early in 1963, Mr. McNamara said:

> What we are proposing is a capability to strike back after absorbing a first blow. This means we have to build and maintain a second strike force. Such a force should have sufficient flexibility to permit a choice of strategies, particularly an ability to: (1) strike back decisively at the entire Soviet target system simultaneously; or (2) strike back first at the Soviet bomber bases, missile sites, and other military installations associated with their long-range nuclear forces to reduce the power of any follow-on attack— and then, if necessary, strike back at the Soviet urban and industrial complex in a controlled and deliberate way.

The Secretary's own testimony, however, seems to make the above strategy highly unlikely. Mr. McNamara went on to say that the Soviets have always insisted that their nuclear power is aimed at the great urban, industrial, and government centers of America; he then stressed the virtual impossibility of either side's destroying the other's hardened* ICBM weapons or Polaris-type submarine missiles. And then the Secretary added a third point, which would seem to remove any real feasibility

---

* "Hardened" means the missile is housed in an underground silo, immune to nearly all attack.

of concentrating our nuclear power on Soviet missile sites rather than cities. In his words: "Furthermore, in a second-strike situation we would be attacking, for the most part, empty sites from which the missiles had already been fired."

It might be reassuring to draw the conclusion from the "no cities" strategy that it is possible to fight a nuclear war centered on destroying missiles rather than people—if only we could build enough missiles to destroy the enemy's nuclear capacity. But anyone who is laboring under the impression that our Defense Department believes this to be feasible should read the congressional testimony of Secretary Mc-Namara of last February. The following brief excerpts from that important 163-page statement should be pondered carefully, especially by the members of Congress who are responsible with the President for the defense policies of our nation:

> Even if we were to double and triple our forces we would not be able to destroy quickly all or almost all of the hardened [Russian] ICBM sites. And even if we could do that, we know no way to destroy the enemy's missile-launching submarines at the same time. We do not anticipate that either the United States or the Soviet Union will acquire that capability in the foreseeable future . . . We could not preclude casualties counted in the tens of millions.
>
> • • •
>
> The expanding arsenals of nuclear weapons on both sides of the Iron Curtain have created an extremely dangerous situation not only for their possessors but also for the world. As the arms race continues and the weapons multiply and become more swift and deadly, the possibility of a global catastrophe, either by miscalculation or design, becomes more real.

Realities of Soviet *versus* American Strengths

I think it is imperative that every American fully understand what our Secretary of Defense has told us. If nuclear war comes—no matter who strikes first—both sides will count their losses in tens of millions of human lives. There is no such condition as true nuclear "superiority" in the sense that either the United States or Russia could escape mass destruction should it attack the other. Neither the U.S. nor the U.S.S.R. can prevent the other from wielding a society-destroying blow, regardless of who attacks first. Under these conditions, the classic military task of defending the shores of our country can no longer be performed.

The Russians do not have a nuclear capacity equal to ours, but our "superiority" is a largely meaningless concept in view of their "relative parity." In the days when warfare was limited to rifles and cannons and tanks and planes, the side with the most weapons and soldiers had a great military advantage. But in the space age, when a nuclear exchange of a few minutes' duration means instant death and indescribable devastation to both sides, what consolation is there to the dazed survivors to know that there remains under the poisoned skies amidst the rubble some unused "overkill" capacity?

When asked at the congressional hearings what the military situation would be after a nuclear exchange between Russia and the United States, Secretary McNamara replied:

> This is a question we have considered. And I can't answer it . . . I think probably . . . the fatalities in western Europe would approach 90 million, the fatalities in the United States would approach 100 million, and the fatalities in the Soviet Union would approach 100 million.
>
> Now when you consider on the order of 300 million people dead in those areas, it is very difficult to conceive of what kind of military weapons . . . would continue to exist. We have nonetheless faced that issue, and we have systems provided that we believe would survive . . .
>
> But it exceeds the extent of my imagination to conceive of how those forces might be used and of what benefit they would be to our nation at that point.

It might be argued by some that our excessive nuclear spending serves an indirect purpose in that it forces the Soviets to strain their less affluent economy to match our effort. But the Russians seem to be avoiding construction of highly sophisticated weapons beyond what they regard as enough to destroy the United States in the event of war.

During the late 1950s when the Soviets could have built hundreds of the latest types of long-range bombers, they constructed less than 200 as against our more than 1,600. There is no indication that they intend to try to narrow this gap. At the present time, while we have a capability of a thousand ICBMs and are building many more, the Russians have built only a minor fraction of that number. Indications are that they will improve and replace rather than greatly increase the number of their missiles.

The question is whether the United States can afford the vast "overkill" capacity that seems to underly much of our military budget.

My own conviction is that we cannot afford this policy economically, politically, or morally, and that if we persist in following it we will weaken our nation both at home and abroad.

No informed person doubts that we have the power to destroy Soviet society several times over. One recent study concluded that we could now erase the bulk of the Russian populace more than a thousand times. Even if that estimate is 100 times too high, we would be able to destroy the Soviet Union with only a partial use of our weapons.

Before the substantial increases in our military power of the past two years, Secretary McNamara testified that "there is no question but that today, our Strategic Retaliatory Forces are fully capable of destroying the Soviet target system, even after absorbing an initial surprise attack."

We have been building missiles, bombs, and other weapons steadily since then, so that our capacity to destroy is much greater than when the Secretary made that statement early in 1962. Speaking of our present capability, Mr. McNamara said on February 6 of 1963: "Allowing for losses from an initial enemy attack and attrition *en route* to target, we calculate that our forces today could still destroy the Soviet Union without any help from the deployed tactical air units or carrier task forces or Thor or Jupiter IRBMs."

Now, I ask what possible advantage there can be to the United States in appropriating additional billions of dollars to build more missiles and bombs when we already have excess capacity to destroy the potential enemy? How many times is it necessary to kill a man or a nation? If the Secretary is correct that one quick nuclear exchange would now leave 100 million Americans dead, an equal number of Russians, and nearly as many west Europeans, is that not enough to deter anyone other than a madman from setting off such a holocaust?

And if either side yields to madness or miscalculation, can any number of arms save us?

A Proposed Arms Budget Adjustment

I think we need to take another careful look at our enormous arms budget, asking ourselves: What part of this budget represents additions to an already surplus overkill capacity? What alternative uses can be made of surplus military funds for strengthening the economic and political foundations of our security?

Our Secretary of Defense has effected many needed economies in operation. Congress can encourage him to make much larger savings by limiting the further pileup of overkill capacity.

After pouring over the complicated tables and charts of the defense budget for hours, I do not pretend to understand all of the implications. Indeed, the data as made available to Congress does not enable one to perceive the full functional pattern proposed. But I am convinced that there is enough talent and brainpower among our military and civilian arms experts to eliminate $5 billion of proposed spending that goes beyond our defense needs.

A front-page story in the Sunday New York *Times* of June 30, 1963, said:

> The administration is giving serious consideration to ordering the first substantial cutback in the production of atomic weapons since the United States began building up its nuclear arsenal after World War II. Behind the current study is a belief that the United States with an

arsenal of tens of thousands of atomic weapons has a sufficient and perhaps an excessive number of nuclear arms to meet its military needs.

The article reported "rising concern in high administration circles over the multiplying number of warheads that have been assigned to the military forces in the last five years. The major fear is that continuing profusion would only increase the chances of accidental explosion or unauthorized use of the weapons." The *Times* reported a growing fear of the members of the Joint Committee on Atomic Energy that the production of atomic weapons is "coming to be based more on the capabilities of the Atomic Energy Commission to manufacture them than on the actual requirements of the military."

The Atomic Energy Commission now has an annual budget of $1.8 billion to produce new warheads to add to our already enormous stockpile. The *Times* asserted that at a recent Pentagon press briefing "a highly placed Defense Department official" estimated that it might be desirable to make a $1 billion cut in this expenditure. Another "policy-making official" said: "We have tens or hundreds of times more weapons than we would ever drop even in an all-out war, and we have had more than we needed for at least two years." None of the sections in this important news article has been challenged by any Administration spokesman—so I think it is safe to assume that they are well-grounded.

I believe that in addition to a cut of $1 billion in the Atomic Energy Commission's weapons procurement program, we could wisely cut an additional $4 billion from the proposed budgets of the air force, navy, and army without reducing the security of the nation. Indeed, such reductions could enable us to strengthen our overall national security. Any such substantial cut should, of course, be applied and administered with the expertise of the Secretary of Defense. I will listen thoughtfully to the presentation of our Appropriations Committee and others. I intend to follow the coming debate and discussion with a frank willingness to change my views if there is compelling contrary evidence.

Planning the Conversion to a Peace Economy

It may be argued that the economy of many of our communities has become so intertwined with military spending that an arms cut of several billion dollars such as I have proposed would result in a painful economic dislocation. Many American communities have come to lean heavily on the economic stimulus of arms production and military installations; we need to accelerate and expand our efforts on the federal, state, and local level to prepare these communities for a conversion to a more permanent economy appropriate to the conditions of peace.

Competence for converting from a military to a civilian economy is a basic requirement for the economic and political security of the United States.

Capability for economic conversion must be developed at all establishments—manufacturing, research, and others—engaged in fulfilling contracts or otherwise working for the Department of Defense or the Atomic Energy Commission.

In order to: minimize dislocation; facilitate industrial expansion; reduce regional dependence on single markets; reduce regional dependence on single government markets; and plan for growth in employment, I recommend the following procedure:

First, all establishments that fulfill Defense Department or Atomic Energy Commission work for at least one calendar year and whose personnel are 25 per cent or more so engaged, should henceforth be required—as a condition of contract fulfillment and acceptable administration—to establish in their managements an operating conversion committee. This committee should actively engage in planning for conversion of the facility from military to civilian work as required in the event of termination, cutbacks, stretchout, or other curtailment of Defense or AEC requirements.

Second, in order to estimate the support that may be required to complement local and regional conversion, an Economic Conversion Commission should be established by the President under the direction of the Secretary of Commerce and including experts from other concerned government departments. Our Arms Control and Disarmament Agency already has a small but able group of people giving thought to this matter.

The Economic Conversion Commission should have responsibility for blueprinting appropriate action by departments and agencies of the federal government that are required to facilitate conversion from a military to a civilian economy.

In addition to such activities as it should deem necessary, the commission would prepare schedules of possible private and public investment patterns and the employment and income effects to be expected therefrom. The information would be reported to the President and to the Congress in preliminary form within six months after the enactment of authorizing legislation and in final form within twelve months.

The commission would take counsel with the governors of all states to encourage appropriate and timely studies and conferences by the states in support of conversion from a military to a civilian economy.

Further, the commission would, within twelve months of establishment, convene a National Conference on Economic Conversion and Growth to focus nationwide attention on the problems of conversion and economic growth and to encourage appropriate study and organization in all relevant parts of the nation's economy. This conference should include invited representatives of trade associations, trade unions, professional societies, representatives of appropriate agencies of the federal and state governments, and selected individuals with specialized knowledge.

With intelligent planning, we can make a satisfactory transition to an economy less dependent upon arms spending.

Weaknesses in an Arms Economy

A closer look at our present level of arms spending will show that it is not an unmixed blessing as a stimulus to our economy.

First of all, we have distorted our economy in allocating such a high percentage of our highly trained manpower, our research and technology, to weapons production, at the expense of our other industry. Japan and our west European allies have all modernized their civilian industrial plant at a much faster rate than the United States, largely because of our concentration on arms production. In this way, our preoccupation with the arms race has added to our civilian production costs, decreased our efficiency, undercut our competitive position in international trade, and aggravated the balance of payments problem.

Building weapons is a seriously limited device for building the economy—partly because it cannot be counted upon as a permanent system and partly because a military item leads to no further production; it is an end in itself. Disarmament chief William C. Foster said recently that "defense spending of the type we now have has no intrinsic merit in terms of its ability to create production and income as compared to other forms of demand."

Many U.S. industries are losing their capacity to compete not only in world trade but also in the United States. The concentration of capital and technical skill in arms production is a basic cause of our declining competitive ability.

As matters now stand, the U.S. government is financing 65 per cent of all research and development and most of that is for military purposes. In Germany, by contrast, 85 per cent of research is privately financed, and nearly all of it is being used to modernize civilian industries, which compete with ours. Those who view military spending as an unmixed blessing to our economy should take a look at the gleaming up-to-date civilian plants in Germany, Belgium, Holland, Italy, and Japan—plants that are surpassing our own neglected civilian production in both quality and low-cost operation. Where will this kind of imbalance leave us in the toughening competition of international trade?

The U.S. economy is jeopardized further by the flow of our gold overseas and the undermining of the dollar as a unit of international exchange. Today, we have a favorable trade balance, but because of our military investments overseas and the flight of investment capital we are suffering an unfavorable balance of payments. Heavy arms spending has aggravated a U.S. fiscal situation that has led many American investors to seek more attractive overseas outlets for their capital.

Our traditionally strong currency has been a powerful instrument in American economic and political leadership in the world. But the strain imposed on our gold reserves as a result of heavy military commitments abroad and excessive arms spending at home is a threat to our international position. The loss of American gold can be halted by reducing some of the burden we have been carrying for the defense of now prosperous allies and by encouraging the conversion of foreign claims on our gold into investments to modernize our industrial system.

While retaining our massive military power, the overriding present need of American security is prompt reinforcement of the economic and political aspects of security at home and abroad.

The Military–Industrial Complex and American Life

It is admittedly difficult to calculate the impact of the arms budget on our civilian economy. It is even more difficult to measure the impact of what former President Eisenhower called "the military–industrial complex" on our moral strength and the climate of freedom. Americans have always feared that any trend toward militarism was a threat to the quality of our democracy; I believe that this is still a legitimate concern. Mr. Eisenhower, whose life had been devoted to military matters, was so concerned about the growing impact of the military–industrial combination on American institutions that he devoted his farewell address to this danger. He warned, "We must never let the weight of this combination endanger our liberties or democratic processes."

Democracy is based on a fundamental respect for the dignity and worth of human life. Its great strength is that it opens the way for the full flowering of man's intellectual, moral and cultural development.

When a major percentage of the public resources of our society is devoted to the accumulation of devastating weapons of war, the spirit of democracy suffers. When our laboratories and our universities and our scientists and our youth are caught up in war preparations, the spirit of free man is hampered.

America must, of course, maintain a fully adequate military defense. But we have a rich heritage and a glorious future that are too precious to risk in an arms race that goes beyond any reasonable criteria of need. We need to remind ourselves that we have sources of strength, of prestige and international leadership based on other than nuclear bombs. Conversely, we need to remember that the greatest communist victories, including the Chinese communist takeover, came at the moment of our greatest nuclear superiority.

The global contest raging before our eyes today will doubtless continue for as long as we can see into the future, but it need not, indeed cannot, be settled by nuclear warfare. The United States must be prepared to lead that contest into areas that draw on our true sources of greatness—politics, economics, and morality. There is a growing indication that the course we follow may play a major part in determining the course that our adversaries take for good or ill.

Our Unmet Public Needs: An Alternative to Overkill

We have millions of idle youth who could be employed in existing job vacancies if only they had sufficient training and education. A sizeable proportion of these are Negroes, and their idleness is at the base of the explosive civil rights crisis now convulsing the nation. What better use could we make of some of our excess military spending than to divert it to an expanded program of vocational and technical training?

Our civil rights problems require for their solution a major expansion of employment opportunity. The economically depressed regions of the country require fresh capital and technical talent. Both these basic problems of economic development require sizeable productive investment.

We have an urgent need for more classrooms, laboratories, libraries and capable teachers; we have millions of citizens, particularly among our older people, who need more adequate hospital and nursing home care. Some of our present defense installations might in the future be converted into vocational schools, community colleges, or health centers.

We have rivers and streams to be saved from pollution and waste—a task calling for considerable engineering and technical manpower. We have a growing number of farm youth who can no longer make an adequate living on the farm whose lives would be enriched by an expanded rural area development effort. And for years to come there will be hungry, afflicted people abroad who look to us for help. Most of the people of the world are undernourished rural families who are trying to scratch an existence from the soil by incredibly primitive methods.

We have an opportunity with our amazing agricultural know-how to use an increased volume of farm products and agricultural assistance as development tools abroad. The recent World Food Congress held in Washington underscored the fact that mankind now has the scientific capacity to eliminate hunger from the world.

I think that we should seriously consider diverting $5 billion of our arms budget into the kind of worthwhile programs at home and abroad I have just sketched. Perhaps some of the military reductions should be expressed in tax reduction. This move would not only result in a stronger and better America, but it might invite a constructive response from the Soviet Union. The Soviets have even more to gain than we from a reduction of military spending: they have deprived themselves of the appliances, automobiles, attractive clothing and other consumer goods that we take for granted.

The cold war is now showing signs of a possible limited thaw. In his inspired address to the nation last Friday evening [July 26, 1963], President Kennedy described in cautious but hopeful terms the larger meaning of the proposed nuclear test ban as a first important step to peace. I trust that after careful consideration the Senate will lend its support to this initiative for peace.

As we weigh the proposed test ban agreement, we can usefully take into account three factors that I have discussed today:

1. When both sides already possess overkill capacity, that lessens the temptation for either side to break the test ban.

2. Some Americans may wonder if the next steps, after a test ban agreement, might not mean declining military spending and a sag in our economy. I am confident that practical steps that I have outlined for preparing and supporting economic conversion will reassure our people on this count.

3. The test ban agreement can lead to savings of many millions of dollars from the funds hitherto used for large-scale testing.

There are hopeful signs other than the proposed test ban. The myth of a solidly united, monolithic communist bloc was long ago thrown in doubt by Tito. But how much more significant is the mounting evidence of a major convulsion of the Sino–Soviet bloc! We should watch these new developments with caution, knowing well that while communist powers may differ with each other, they continue to follow a tyrannical system that is alien to American democracy. But we must also keep free from a rigid diplomacy or excessive reliance on arms that might jeopardize our capacity to exploit for peace these fast-developing changes in the international climate.

Thirteen years ago in March, 1950, the late Senator Brien McMahon, chairman of the Joint Committee on Atomic Energy, made two memorable addresses from the floor of the Senate. The Connecticut senator warned that a continuance of the arms race would lead sooner or later to catastrophe, and in any event would induce a climate of fear and a government-controlled allocation of resources that would dry up the well-springs of American freedom and dignity. The senator concluded with this warning:

> Mr. President, the clock is ticking, ticking, and with each swing of the pendulum the time to save civilization grows

shorter. When shall we get about this business? Now, or when Russia and the United States glower at one another from atop competing stacks of hydrogen bombs?

We have arrived at the point in history where we indeed "glower at one another from atop competing stacks of hydrogen bombs." And if the present trend continues, in a few short years a half dozen and then a dozen new powers will climb atop their hydrogen stockpiles to glower at their frightened neighbors.

The clock Senator McMahon heard ticking in 1950 is still ticking; our ears have become so accustomed to the sound that we scarcely hear it. Yet, scientists of our day flatly assert that if we do not reverse the arms race, a major nuclear accident will occur before this decade ends even without the intent of the nuclear powers. And how can we rest secure, knowing that any one of three, six, or a dozen national defense ministries or subordinate military officers could set off a nuclear holocaust through miscalculation, impulsive madness, or simply human wickedness.

There are powerful options of peace as well as options of war. Still alive in the world is a faith that can move mountains if we will only seize upon it. From our own heritage the philosophy of Jefferson and Lincoln speak with a voice that is more effectively heard in Asia, Africa, and Latin America than any number of nuclear explosions or moon shots. A conscientious effort on our part to eliminate excessive nuclear stockpiling will give that voice of peace and reason an even clearer tone.

■ *Although I knew the Senate was unlikely to accept the proposal of a $5 billion cut in arms spending I made on August 2, 1963, or any similar proposal from a first year senator, I took the Senate floor the following month to plead again for a first step in reversing the arms race. I presented an amendment to reduce arms spending by $2.2 billion—a 10 per cent cut in the Appropriations Committee's recommended funds for military procurement, research and development. This amendment, on a roll call vote requested by Senator Barry Goldwater, gained only two votes: my own, and that of Senator Jennings Randolph of West Virginia, who was anxious to divert additional federal funds to his economically depressed Appalachian constituency.*

The following speech, delivered on the Senate floor in September of 1963, in support of my amendment, centers mainly on the need to reverse the arms race, but it also includes what I believe was the first opposition on the senate floor to our military involvement in Vietnam. Subsequent events bore out the essential soundness of the views in this speech, which served to convince me that a senator should act from his convictions even though he knows the chances of acceptance are not immediately favorable.

In more recent years, increasing numbers of senators have reached the conviction that substantial savings can and should be made in military spending by such steps as removing or at least sharply reducing the 300,000 U.S. troops in western Europe, rejecting the proposed fast-deployment naval ship and the A-7 aircraft, stopping the proposed anti-ballistic missile system, and reducing military foreign aid.

A Proposal to Reverse the Arms Race

AMERICAN SECURITY IN A CHANGING WORLD

The late James Thurber, writing in the *New Yorker Magazine in 1956, related the following fable:*

One morning the tiger woke up in the jungle and told his mate that he was king of beasts.

"Leo, the lion, is king of beasts," replied his mate.

"We need a change," said the tiger. "The creatures are crying for a change. . . . I'll be king of beasts by the time the moon rises . . . It will be a yellow moon with black stripes, in my honor."

The tiger prowled through the jungle till he came to the lion's den. "Come out," he roared, "and greet the king of beasts!"

"I am the king of beasts," roared Leo, and he charged out of the den to defend his crown against the pretender.

It was a terrible fight, and it lasted until the setting of the sun. All the animals of the jungle joined in, some taking the side of the tiger and others the side of the lion. Every creature from the aardvark to the zebra took part in the struggle to overthrow the lion or to repulse the tiger, and some did not know which they were fighting for, and some fought for both, and some fought whoever was nearest, and some fought for the sake of fighting.

"What are we fighting for?" someone asked the aardvark.

"The old order," said the aardvark.

"What are we dying for?" someone asked the zebra.

Speech in the United States Senate, September 24, 1963.

"The new order," said the zebra.

When the moon rose, fevered and gibbous, it shone upon a jungle in which nothing stirred except a macaw and a cockatoo, screaming in horror. All the beasts were dead except the tiger, and his days were numbered and his time was ticking away. He was monarch of all he surveyed, but it didn't seem to mean anything.

MORAL: You can't very well be king of beasts if there aren't any.

Thurber's fable is broadly applicable to our human condition. The point at which the parallel is least exact is that the animal kingdom has not yet found the secret of total destruction, whereas man has mastered this knowledge and achieved the means of applying it on a global scale.

Thanks to the oppressive political policies of the European dictators, which caused the world's greatest scientists to seek freedom in the United States during the 1930s, we were the first nation to discover and use an atomic weapon. Since that day at Hiroshima eighteen years ago, there has never been any real doubt about man's capacity for universal destruction.

For several years we held an atomic monopoly. There are no lasting secrets in the world of science, however, and presently the Soviet Union tested an atomic device. Since then, she has proceeded to build and explode the world's biggest hydrogen bomb. No one doubts the capacity of many other nations to join the nuclear club in the next few years.

We do not know the exact size of the nuclear stockpiles in the opposing camps of today. The most painstaking assessments run from the equivalent of 40 to 60 billion tons of TNT. This means that there is potentially a ten- or twenty-ton bomb ticking at the head of every boy and girl, of every man and woman, on the face of the earth.

Our most trusted scientists and military authorities have no doubt that either the United States or the Soviet Union can destroy the other several times over. Both President Kennedy and Secretary McNamara have publicly warned that no matter who strikes first, a sixty-minute nuclear exchange between Russia and America would leave over half the people dead in both countries. Chairman Khrushchev added in a warning note to Peking that the resulting misery and despair would cause "the survivors to envy the dead."

Is there any one of us in this Senate chamber who can really contemplate the prospect of survival in the midst of 300 million corpses—with the cathedrals, the museums, the art galleries, the libraries, the universities—all of these depositories of mankind's dreams and achievements of thousands of years reduced to radioactive dust in a few moments of madness.

We have learned to live in the shadow of extinction primarily because we believe that no nation would dare use its nuclear arsenal lest it bring on its own destruction.

In one of his colorful phrases, Winston Churchill described the situation after the first Soviet atomic explosion in 1949 as: "Peace through mutual terror." As Churchill put it, "safety will become the sturdy child of terror; and survival the twin brother of annihilation."

Churchill's eloquent phrasing was distinctive, but his theory was not. On March 27, 1880, Dr. J. H. McLean, a St. Louis industrialist, demonstrated his breech-loading, repeating cannon to a group of reporters. Naming his invention "The Annihilator," Dr. McLean asserted: "The art of war will be no more in a few years! Terrible perfection shall make wars impossible . . . I have an invention which will perfect warfare, the perfection being to prevent war by making it terrible."

The repeating cannon did indeed make wars "terrible," but not so terrible as to prevent two world conflicts and a dozen lesser ones.

Prior to Dr. McLean's "Annihilator," Alfred Nobel, the European munitions manufacturer, longed "to turn out a substance or a machine of such horrible capacity for mass annihilation that thereby wars would become altogether impossible."

Nobel thought he had achieved his goal in 1864 when he developed dynamite, but seven years later the new dynamite bombs were hurled into the Franco–Prussian war with no apparent contribution to the cause of world peace.

There is nothing in the historical record to assure us that

awesome weapons of death can safeguard the peace. Admittedly, atomic weapons have introduced an unprecedented dimension to warfare, but as William H. Honan has pointed out:

> Mankind settled for itself the question of whether or not to use this weapon eighteen years ago at Hiroshima when the user, it should be remembered, was not backed against a wall, but was within sight of victory. Nuclear weapons, like all of their predecessors, will have their day. The only question is: When next?

I believe that the United States, for many reasons, has a unique responsibility to lead the world back from the nuclear abyss to make certain that nuclear weapons do not "have their day."

In a speech to the Senate on August 2, entitled "New Perspectives on American Security," I called for a reconsideration of some of the basic postulates on which our present security and defense policies rest. Today, we have before us the military appropriations bill for the current fiscal year. When the remaining military items not included in this bill are acted on in the near future, we will have passed judgment on a total military budget well in excess of $50 billion.

Neither the judgment of the legislative committees nor the special competence of the Defense Department releases any senator from his individual responsibility to follow his convictions on an issue so important as the bill now before us. What we are evaluating now is not simply a military weapons system. The size of this proposed appropriation is so great that in approving or rejecting or modifying it, we are to a considerable degree determining the priorities of our national life. This is a judgment not for military experts alone, but for the entire nation acting through the President and the elected representatives of the fifty states. Each one of us must weigh the military, economic, international and moral issues involved and then vote his convictions.

The senator from Georgia, Mr. Russell, said during the recent test ban debate that he would not hesitate to speak and vote his convictions even if he stood all alone against the judgment of his colleagues and the administration. Our constituents have a right to expect that kind of individual conviction and courage from each senator.

We owe the nation a full-scale public discussion and debate on this largest of all appropriations bills to come before the Congress. Some months ago we engaged in hours of intensive debate on the question of whether we could afford to spend a hundred million dollars for a youth conservation and training program. A few weeks ago we debated at great length and engaged in a series of closely fought roll calls to decide whether or not we should provide the same protection for American workers that we give to imported Mexican braceros. We debated intensely both in the House and in the Senate the question of providing less than $200 million to meet the mental health needs of the nation. Yet, in recent years, enormous expenditures for armaments have slipped through almost without raising a question on the Senate floor.

This practice was described in the Bible centuries ago as "straining at a gnat and swallowing a camel."

Earlier I proposed to the Senate that we reduce our arms budget by $5 billion—a $1 billion cut in the Atomic Energy Commission weapons acquisition budget and a $4 billion reduction of the Defense Department's military budget. I am all the more certain today that this $5 billion savings in arms spending would be justified—that far from weakening us, it would give new vigor and health to the nation.

I believe that the cut ought to be made now and not postponed at the expense of such other desirable goals as the education of our children and the development of our rural and urban life.

Five billion dollars will not buy very many aircraft carriers or supersonic bombers or nuclear submarines, but it would build a $1 million school in every one of the nation's 3,000 counties, plus 500 hospitals costing $1 million apiece, plus college scholarships worth $5,000 each to 100,000 students— and still permit a tax reduction of a billion dollars. Or, turning our attention abroad, just 1/10 of that saving would finance our entire commitment to the Alliance for Progress this year.

The Senate committee has already cut over $1.5 billion dollars from the Administration's proposed defense budget. As I have indicated, another $1 billion can and should be cut from the AEC weapons program when that budget is presented to us. An additional half a billion can and should be cut from the $1.5 billion foreign military aid budget when that bill is under consideration. This leaves a balance of $2 billion to complete the $5 billion total reduction that I have suggested.

I propose and send to the desk an amendment providing for a 10 per cent cut in the procurement and the research and development portions of the bill pending. This would result in a reduction of approximately $1.5 billion in the procurement of weapons and approximately $700 million in research and development. (More exactly: a 10 per cent cut would mean a reduction of $1,579,544,700 in the committee's recommended $15,795,447,000 for procurement and a reduction of $698,423,000 in the committee recommendation of $6,984,230,000 for research and development.)

I believe this modest reduction is justified, first of all, because our country already has sufficient nuclear power to deter or retaliate against any likely enemy action. Also, in the last two years we have greatly strengthened our conventional war capability. Indeed, a major portion of the $10 billion increase in military spending over the last Eisenhower budget has gone into conventional warfare capability and special forces.

Nearly two years ago, Secretary McNamara expressed the conviction that we had more than enough nuclear weapons to destroy the enemy even after absorbing a first strike. Mr. McNamara's judgment was supported by one of our noted nuclear authorities, whose book published at that time concluded that the U.S. nuclear arsenal was then one and a half million times as powerful as the bomb that wiped out Hiroshima.

Since then we have poured additional billions into our strategic retaliatory system.

I realize that our growing number of military theorists have devised an endless number of alternative strategies designed to justify this vast "overkill" capacity. But Senator Russell said on April 11, 1962, in commenting on the growing number of nuclear strategies and refinements: "I have no hesitancy in saying . . . that to me these extrapolations, or projections, or hypotheses are exceedingly unrealistic. In my opinion, if nuclear war begins, it would be a war of extermination." There is no convincing refutation to the words of the senator from Georgia.

The nation does not need a special nuclear system to cover the strategy of every theorist employed at the Pentagon. We do need the capacity to deter an attack—which means enough to destroy the enemy even after absorbing a first strike. We have been well beyond that capability for at least two years, as the Defense Department would readily agree. Yet the bill now before us calls for additional billions to add new force and refinements to our retaliatory power. A significant portion of the procurement expense in this proposed appropriation is for more missiles. A heavy part of the proposed research and development is aimed at new styles of nuclear devices—medium-range mobile missiles, tactical nuclear artillery, and a bewildering array of sophisticated, highly expensive modifications.

Over half a billion dollars is included in this bill for battlefield tactical nuclear devices. We already have 10,000 nuclear weapons in Europe, which is enough to ensure the death of the Continent if war should come. Actually, these weapons are a threat to our security rather than a safeguard. Their presence in Europe almost guarantees that any conflict that develops there will escalate into a nuclear exchange between Russia and ourselves. As they proliferate, we increase the risk that one of them may one day set off a conflagration that could destroy western society. Adding hundreds of millions of dollars to this tactical nuclear weapons force is literally courting disaster—and wasting an enormous volume of tax dollars.

But the weight of argument today, as in my August 2 statement, does not center on competing weapons systems. Rather, I am pleading for an overall reduction in military spending on the grounds that we already possess sufficient power to deter the enemy and meet our other military needs.

Let no one suggest that if my amendment to cut $2 billion plus from this bill is approved, it will threaten our security. We will still have, with the inclusion of the AEC weapons program and other military items to be considered subsequently, a total arms budget of $50 billion. We will still have the world's mightiest bomber force—some 700 B-52s and B-58s and several hundred B-47s. We have already provided funds for $1,000 intercontinental ballistic missiles and 35 Polaris submarines carrying 560 missiles. Any single one of these several thousand nuclear delivery systems is capable of unleashing more explosive power than all the explosives of World War Two. Any single bomb or warload on the fantastic stockpiles that we have been building for eighteen years would make the killer of Hiroshima look like a child's toy.

The hard-bitten realists in the Kremlin know that if they were to attack the United States, their country would be utterly destroyed. Knowing this grim fact, they have not, according to our best information attempted to outstrip the United States either in bombers in the late 1950s or in missiles in the 1960s. Indeed, the Russians have only a fraction of the airpower and missile strength of the United States. Every indication is that they are modifying and replacing rather than greatly increasing their nuclear delivery system.

I sometimes think that our military theorists may be running a race with each other rather than with the Russians.

If we are building up a larger weapons system than we need for military security, that is reason enough to justify the modest cut I have proposed. But there is a second reason: our excessive military spending is leading to the neglect of other vital sources of national strength.

Of an estimated 400,000 scientists and engineers engaged in research and development in this country, only 120,000, according to the Department of Commerce, are devoted to civilian activities. The *Wall Street Journal* of August 9, 1963, reported that "there is solid evidence that the shortage of scientific talent is slowing private research," and further, that:

> Top research men in industry reason this way: Frantic bidding, by space and military contractors, for scientists and engineers, is creating a big shortage for industry. This

scarcity, along with the skyrocketing salaries it is provoking, is bringing almost to a halt the hitherto rapid growth of company-supported research. This development hampers efforts to develop new products and processes for the civilian economy.

The concentration of technical talent in the military sphere has been impairing the competitive position of American industry in relation to other major industrial countries. The Chamber of Commerce of the United States, in a statement before the Joint Economic Committee of the Congress, pointed out that:

> . . . in terms of the proportion of its available research and development talent devoted to industry and commerce, the U.S. effort is only half of that of West Germany. This is a potential cause of lagging employment and deterrent to increasing productivity . . . Should not national policies recognize the national importance of a sound and prosperous national economy as weighted against the prestige value of space exploration or "overkill" in military defense?

Evidence of industrial depletion is found at critical points in our manufacturing industry, notably, machinery production. The United States, long a world leader in the design and production of basic metal-working machine tools, is now in a declining position in this basic industry. The United States now has the distinction of operating the oldest stock of metal-working machinery of any major industrial country. Once first in quantity in the world, our machine-tool production now ranks fourth or fifth. Our capacity to compete in international trade and our balance of payment position are seriously weakened by this neglect of our civilian industry.

The depletion of education for our young people is one of the heavy prices we are paying for draining off our competent young men and women into military technical work. A mechanical engineer with ten years' experience earns $11,500 a year, on the average, in the aerospace industries. In civilian work, his counterpart earns $9,300. The teachers in our schools average about half the salary of these industry technicians. As a result, even in our prosperous metropolitan suburbs, thousands of teachers employed in the public schools are unable to meet reasonable teaching standards. The use of substandard teachers means substandard education. Thereby, we are shortchanging our young people and, indeed, our entire society.

Not only are we starving certain essential sources of national strength because of our heavy military spending; we are also neglecting important aspects of the international challenge.

The contest with international communism cannot be won in the military arena. Indeed, the true "no win" policy is one that depends too heavily on armaments. If we ever have to use our nuclear weapons, it will mean that both we and the Soviets have lost the contest. There can be no victor in mutual annihilation.

The current dilemma in Vietnam is a clear demonstration of the limitations of military power. There in the jungles of Asia, our mighty nuclear arsenal—our $50 billion arms budget —our costly new "special forces"—have proved powerless to cope with a ragged band of illiterate guerrillas fighting with homemade weapons.

We cannot even persuade a government financed and armed by American taxpayers from tyrannizing its citizens and throwing insults at our President when he objects. Although we have spent $3 billion on the Vietnam war, lost many lives, and are continuing to spend $2 million dollars daily, the liberties of the Vietnamese people are not expanding. Instead, we find them harassed, not only by terrorists in the countryside, but also by official government troops in the cities. We find American money and arms used to suppress the very liberties we went in to defend.

This is scarcely a policy of "victory"; it is not even a policy of "stalemate." It is a policy of moral debacle and political defeat. It is a policy that demonstrates that our expenditures for more and more "special forces" are as useless and dangerous as our expenditures for more and more nuclear capability.

The failure of our Vietnam policy should be a signal for every one of us in this chamber to re-examine the roots of that policy. Part of those roots are here before us today in the excessive portion of the military appropriations bill; and we stand derelict before history if we fail to make the examination. For the failure in Vietnam will not remain confined to Vietnam. The trap we have fallen into there will haunt us in every corner of this revolutionary world if we do not properly appraise its lessons.

I submit that America will exert a far greater impact for peace and freedom in Asia and elsewhere if we rely less on armaments and more on the economic, political, and moral sources of our strength.

We spent less on the entire Peace Corps than we do on a Polaris submarine. Yet, this band of idealistic American youth have demonstrated around the world the mighty power of a good idea, of willing hands and a warm heart.

As the former director of the nation's Food for Peace Program, I can testify to the enormous contribution American agricultural abundance is making to peace and freedom. We live in a hungry world that is torn between the appeals of communism and democracy. In that contest, our greatest material advantage is not our nuclear stockpile, but the amazing productivity of the American farmer. Is there any doubt that Mr. Khrushchev would exchange any asset he has to secure America's food-producing capacity? Is there any doubt that if he had our agricultural surpluses, he would use them as economic and political instruments in the global contest of our time?

Hunger is the companion of communism; food is freedom's first line of defense. I think we need to continue to expand and improve our Food for Peace Program so long as there is a hungry child crying for food anywhere on the face of the earth.

As a former combat pilot, I know the need for a strong military force. But let us never sell short the power of the democratic ideal. Let us not underestimate the capacity of the American economy to engage in a growing commerce with the family of nations when it is geared up for that purpose rather than war. Let us not overlook the mighty power of a nation that draws on deep sources of moral and spiritual strength. Let us live more with faith and less with fear.

Finally, I ask for support for this modest proposal to reduce the arms budget because I think it may help to reverse the arms race.

The test ban treaty may prove to be an historic step away from war toward peace. I do not base my proposed amendment on the treaty. It is justified by its own merit. But I do hope that like the partial ban on nuclear explosions, it may take us another step away from the abyss. It may induce a counter arms reduction by the Soviet Union.

What I am suggesting here is that we employ in reverse order the same factors of action and reaction which feed an arms race. I was startled a few months ago when I read the testimony of Secretary McNamara to see how graphically he revealed the nature of the arms race. In explaining how we plan our budget and weapons systems to counter the Soviet threat, Mr. McNamara said: "We are, in effect, attempting to anticipate production and deployment decisions which our opponents themselves may not yet have made." We can assume, I think, that just as we try to counter the growing weapons budget of the Soviet Union, so do they try to evaluate and predict our next move.

An Englishman once remarked: "We ought to build our navy up to double the size of theirs if they build theirs up to the point they say they will if we build ours up." That is the arms race in a nutshell. But it is far more dangerous today than it was in the nineteenth century world of the Englishman.

The nuclear arms race is a dead-end street. It creates a "balance of terror" that at best leaves us warped by fear and at worst destroys us all.

Is it possible that our country can take the lead in a cautious effort to move the world back step by step from the precipice of death?

■ *Few debates in the history of the Senate have honored the best traditions of that body more than the discussion centering on ratification of the limited nuclear test ban.*

On July 25, 1963, six weeks after President Kennedy's announcement that the United States was halting its testing of nuclear weapons in the atmosphere, Averill Harriman, representing the United States, Lord Hailsham, for the British, and Chairman Khrushchev, signed an agreement in Moscow to end the atmospheric testing of nuclear weapons. The following day in a televised address to the American people, the President hailed the test ban agreement as "a shaft of light" that had "cut into the darkness."

There remained, however, a hard fight in the Senate, where a two-thirds majority vote was required for ratification of the proposed treaty. Opposition to the agreement centered, first, on the contention that future U.S. nuclear superiority required unlimited testing, and secondly, on the claim that the test ban would prevent the development of an antimissile missile.

The proponents of the treaty, supported by assurances from some of the nation's top scientific and military experts, were able to counter these arguments successfully in several weeks of constructive, usually intelligent debate. The result on September 24, 1963, was an overwhelming vote for ratification, 80–19—fourteen more than the required two-thirds.

The Nuclear
Test Ban Treaty

I support the nuclear test ban treaty without reservation. The weeks of committee hearings—the supporting statements of our top government, scientific, military and religious leaders—the specific endorsements by the President, the Secretary of State, the Secretary of Defense, the Joint Chiefs of Staff— all of these have only served to fortify my convictions as to the logic of the treaty.

The Senate and the nation were further strengthened in their support for the test ban by the eloquent statement of Majority Leader Mansfield and by the speech of Minority Leader Dirksen, whose plea to the Senate was one of the most moving I have ever witnessed. Senator Fulbright, the chairman of the Senate Foreign Relations Committee, has likewise set forth what seems to me to be an irrefutable argument for approval of the treaty.

In his news conference of last Thursday, President Kennedy summarized the case for ratification when he said:

This treaty will enable all of us who inhabit the earth, our children and our children's children, to breathe easier, free from the fear of nuclear test fallout. It will curb the spread of nuclear weapons to other countries, thereby holding out hope for a more peaceful and stable world.

It will slow down the nuclear arms race impairing the adequacy of this nation's arsenal or security, and it will offer a small but important foundation on which a world of law can be built.

Speech in the United States Senate, September 16, 1963.

Radiation Hazard of Nuclear Testing

I am for this ban on atmospheric testing first of all because I am worried by the danger to our children, and to generations yet unborn, of death-dealing radioactive fallout.

Early Saturday morning, the world thrilled to the news that five apparently healthy babies were born to Mr. and Mrs. Andrew Fischer of Aberdeen, South Dakota. As the junior senator from South Dakota, I share the special pride South Dakotans draw from this blessed and remarkable event.

If the quintuplets survive, and we pray that they will, they will be the first quintuplets to survive in the history of our country. Their birth reminds us again of the miracle and the glory of life. Medical science will surely be available to give the Fischer children every needed attention and care.

I have been searching for some concrete gesture I could offer to assist this wonderful family that now totals twelve. Perhaps there is no greater gift that I can offer as one of the elected representatives of this family than to work in every possible way for a world where these children, all the children of South Dakota, indeed, all the children of the earth, can breathe clean air and live free from the blight of hatred and war.

It is true that the experts do not agree about the number of leukemia or cancer victims there may be if we do not cease polluting the air with test explosions. We do not yet know for certain how much genetic damage may be done to the brains, the bones, and the tissue of the children of the future if the nuclear test explosions continue. But we do know that uncontrolled testing with more and more nations joining in the nuclear race will doom thousands of innocent human beings to suffering and death.

Harvard's distinguished professor of biology, Matthew Meselson, told the Senate Foreign Relations Committee that "a reasonable estimate for the number of children with gross mental or physical defects who will be born in the world because of the genetic effects of fallout from tests conducted to date is about 50,000." Recent government surveys have reported radioactive concentrations in some localities two or three times greater than we had previously believed to exist. The tragic fact is that we may not know for another generation or more the full effect of radiation damage already caused by nuclear explosions.

The Friday issue of the Washington *Star* carried an urgent half-page paid advertisement sponsored by the noted physician, Benjamin Spock, and sixty-six other medical doctors:

> We believe that as a result of the fallout from past tests, at best a small percentage of our children will develop cancer or leukemia in the future, and that some of our children's children will be born with physical deformities or mental deficiencies. If testing in the atmosphere continues, the risks will increase.

Some persons have contended that the radiation danger is a minor factor since it may affect only a small percentage of the world's children. But if one of those children happened to be yours or mine, we would not think that was a minor matter. No one of us relishes the thought of living permanently with the fear that our families might be drinking contaminated milk or eating polluted food or breathing poisonous air.

But we would have less cause to complain about radiation damage to one of our children as a result of nuclear testing than would a parent in Norway or Tunisia or the Philippines. For we have a voice and a vote in the determination of the nuclear policy of the world's mightiest nation—the first nation to develop and explode a nuclear device. Those millions of human beings around the world who are nervously watching the nuclear race must rest their chances of survival on what the giant powers decide to do. Like the rain, radioactive dust falls alike on the just and the unjust, the innocent and the guilty, the weak and the strong. Little wonder, then, that some ninety-one nations have quickly offered their signatures to the treaty now pending before the Senate. This one single factor —the radiation hazard—places a sobering responsibility on those who say that we will all be safer if the nations of the world continue to explode their nuclear warheads in the air.

Of course, those who oppose the treaty contend that we must risk radioactive fallout to avoid the military risk involved in the limited test ban. I think this argument has been demolished by our best military and scientific authorities—to say nothing of the moral, political, and diplomatic issues involved.

We now have a clear-cut nuclear superiority over any other nation. We have enough warheads and delivery systems right now to obliterate civilization even if we never test another bomb or missile. Far from adding to our nuclear superiority, continued testing by ourselves and other countries could clear the way for our rivals to narrow our nuclear lead.

There are those who argue that we need to test in the atmosphere to develop a defensive anti-missile missile. This argument falters at two points: (1) it is highly unlikely that either we or the Russians can develop any really dependable defense against offensive missiles; (2) the unsolved problems of the anti-missile missile do not call for atmospheric testing but relate instead to technical problems such as guidance systems and the identification of incoming missiles.

The only dependable protection against enemy missiles is the enemy's knowledge that if he destroys our country, we can destroy his simultaneously. We are in a balance of terror today and neither side has the slightest need to explode another test bomb to demonstrate its killing power. The leaders of both the United States and Russia already know that a nuclear exchange of a few minutes' duration would incinerate most of the people in both nations. If that is not enough to deter a nuclear strike, then mankind is doomed no matter how many test bombs we explode or fail to explode.

But for those in doubt, we have the repeated assurance of our President and our military leaders that underground testing will be energetically pushed and that we will be prepared to resume atmospheric tests if that becomes necessary. Indeed, Mr. President, the Administration has been called upon to give so many assurances of our continued nuclear efforts after treaty ratification that a casual observer might assume that we are approving this treaty so that we can accelerate the arms race and beef up the war-making facilities of our country! There seems to be a side of our nature that leads us to require repeated assurances that we will continue to add to our capacity to annihilate the enemy more thoroughly than he annihilates us.

Some spokesmen have warned about the great danger of "euphoria" setting in if we cease exploding test bombs over the heads of the earth's inhabitants. Webster defines "euphoria" as "bodily comfort; a feeling of well-being."

Frankly, I think there is less danger to the world from this dread disease, "euphoria," with its symptoms of "bodily comfort" and "a feeling of well-being," than from polluting the air with radiation and accelerating the nuclear race.

As a former combat soldier I know the necessity of a strong and alert national defense. But I also know that there is more to the defense of a nation than the size of its nuclear stockpile. We need to balance off the alleged danger of becoming afflicted by "a feeling of well-being" against the dangers to our way of life from another ten, twenty, or fifty years of mounting tension, anxiety, and fear. What does it do to a free society to live decade after decade under the shadow of a nuclear armaggedon? What does it do to our nation to invest annually more than half of our entire national budget in building the weapons of death, while neglecting the quality of our schools, our cities, and our lives?

I fully agree with Louisiana's Senator Ellender, who said on Friday: "If the Senate should fail to ratify the test ban treaty, it appears to me we face two alternatives, and either will be destructive of our way of life. We may eventually drift or be forced into a nuclear war with Russia or we will go broke attempting to maintain the status quo indefinitely. Does any intelligent person believe we can continue to pour out between $50 and $60 billion for any length of time without doing violence and much harm to our economy and our way of life? I, for one, do not." Senator Ellender expressed the hope of a world that longs for peace when he said that the treaty could be a first step to thaw the cold war and help dispel the fear existing between Russia and the United States.

This brings me to one aspect of the treaty ratification that I think has not had sufficient consideration. I refer to the impact of this "first step" upon the communist world.

The Treaty and the Sino–Soviet Rift

All of us would readily agree that the hopes for world peace depend not only on the policy of the United States, but even more significantly on the course the communist world follows. All of our hopes for peace could be dashed into a nuclear holocaust no matter what we do if the Soviets and their allies decide that they prefer that alternative to co-existence. So we need to consider whether ratification of the test ban encourages the forces of peace or war in the communist sectors of the globe.

During most of the eighteen years since World War Two, we have thought of the communist nations as a monolithic structure solidly united under the leadership of Moscow. With the emergence of a communist regime in Peking, we developed the phrase "Sino–Soviet bloc" to describe what we believed to be the common front of Russian and Chinese communist power. We noted and partially exploited the divergence of Tito's Yugoslavia from Moscow leadership, but we saw this as a unique and uncertain exception to the monolithic nature of international communism.

In recent years, however, we have witnessed a fast-growing split in the Sino–Soviet bloc. Indeed, there is now clear evidence of a bitter power struggle between Moscow and Peking for leadership of international communism. *The New Cold War: Moscow versus Peking* is the title of a newly published book by Edward Crankshaw, the London *Observer*'s respected authority on Soviet affairs. Crankshaw sees the first signs of the Russo-Chinese rift in the notable twentieth party congress of February, 1956, when Khrushchev launched the movement to downgrade Stalin. At the same congress, Khrushchev announced that war with the capitalist societies is no longer considered inevitable in communist dogma; the Chinese took issue with both of these developments.

For several years the Soviets and the Chinese tried to soften the public demonstration of their differences by indirect verbal attacks. When the Chinese wanted to attack the views of Moscow they did so by sharp criticism of Yugoslavia. The Russians would reply by a verbal blast at Albania.

There are numerous factors involved in the widening Sino–Soviet rift. Basically, however, the dispute centers around Khrushchev's policy of co-existence and accommodation with the west. While Mr. Khrushchev has given growing evidence of his desire to avoid a military showdown, the Chinese have denounced this policy as a cowardly betrayal of communist principle.

During 1959, Khrushchev seemed to be cultivating President Eisenhower and laying the groundwork through the "spirit of Camp David" for a high-level understanding. The subsequent summit conference in Paris in the spring of 1960 was, however, torpedoed by the ill-fated U-2 incident and Khrushchev's violent reaction. It seems probable that the "hard-liners" in the Kremlin and in Peking made it politically necessary for Khrushchev to back off from the Paris conference when the U-2 incident erupted on the very eve of the conference. Since that time, the Soviet leader has seemed to act alternately belligerent and peaceful, but he has always backed away from the much more aggressive course demanded by Peking.

The Moscow–Peking battle broke into full public view following the Cuban missile crisis of last October. After gambling on the missile installations in Cuba, which he thought would strengthen his hand for a showdown on Berlin, Khrushchev withdrew his missiles in the face of President Kennedy's stern ultimatum. This withdrawal infuriated the Chinese, who saw it as a surrender to the hated imperialists—the United States, which had previously been described by Peking as a "paper tiger." "The paper tiger has nuclear teeth," Khrushchev said. He warned the Chinese that to follow the unyielding militaristic course advocated by them would lead to a nuclear devastation that would cause survivors to "envy the dead."

The Moscow–Peking differences were further inflamed by the Chinese attack on the Indian border, which coincided with the Cuban missile crisis. Moscow made no effort to hide its displeasure, and in fact assisted the Indians rather than its communist ally. This summer the world has witnessed an exchange of lengthy letters between the Communist Parties of China and Russia that erase any doubt about the fundamental ideological conflict between the two countries.

No one can read the article on the origins of the Sino–Soviet rift published by Peking on September 6 without sensing the intensity of the struggle. The article traces the dispute to the Twentieth Congress of the Communist Party of the Soviet Union in 1956 and the Soviet peaceful co-existence policy that accompanied the downgrading of Stalin. The Peking government takes strong exception to the Soviet warning about the necessity of avoiding a nuclear war.

In its letter to Peking on July 14 this year, the Central Committee of the Soviet Communist Party wrote:

> The Communist Party of the Soviet Union Central Committee believes it a necessary duty to tell the party and the people with all frankness that in questions of war and peace the Chinese Communist Party leadership is based on principle differences with us, with the world communist movement. The essence of these differences lies in the diametrically opposite approach to such vital problems as the possibility of averting a world thermonuclear war, peaceful co-existence of states with different social systems, and interconnection between the struggle for peace and the development of the world revolutionary movement.

Two recent actions of the Soviet Union point up their acute differences with Peking. Under Secretary of State Averell Harriman has noted that it was the U.S.S.R. that proposed that the successful test ban treaty negotiations should begin in Moscow on July 15; previously, July 5 had been fixed for the Moscow talks with the Chinese. The Soviet letter from which I have quoted was sent on July 14, while talks with the Chinese communists were in progress. Both the timing of these events and the substance of that letter are less than conciliatory toward the Chinese.

The Chinese communists have denounced the proposed test ban as a "nuclear fraud," a "fake peace," an instrument of nuclear "monopoly," and a "capitulation to U.S. imperialism" that allows it to "gain military superiority." In the history of the Sino–Soviet dispute published by Peking on September 6, the Chinese berated Moscow for scrapping its agreement to help China develop nuclear weapons. Peking said that the agreement was broken "apparently as a gift" to President Eisenhower "to curry favor with the U.S. imperialists" during the Khrushchev visit to the United States in September, 1959.

One could quote at length from the growing literature of dispute, down to the recent bitter exchange about incidents along the frontier between the U.S.S.R. and communist China and the charge by Peking that Mr. Khrushchev has joined President Kennedy, President Tito, and Prime Minister Nehru as a "vaudeville star" in a new Holy Alliance. What I have said, however, is quite enough to remind the Senate that this dispute is a major reason for Soviet agreement to the treaty. Some of our most able Soviet authorities, including Mr. Harriman, believe that Mr. Khrushchev urgently needs some tangible evidence that his doctrine of peaceful co-existence is a more practical policy than the militant Chinese line. The treaty is popular in eastern Europe, where there is pressure for more independence from Soviet control. It has been widely acclaimed by the developing countries of the globe. It is plausible that Moscow desires the treaty to win greater voluntary support among people both at home and abroad. Khrushchev doubtless feels that he can command greater influence by supporting the test ban as a symbol of peace than Mao can in the role of an unyielding warmonger.

Beyond this, it is quite probable that the Soviet leadership should mean in a literal sense what they say about avoiding nuclear holocaust even as they say it for political effect. Why should they not wish to avoid a nuclear war that could destroy most of their country? Why should it not be reasonable to suppose that in the avoidance of nuclear war at least, we have some common ground with them; that they conceive of this treaty, as we do, as a step—admittedly a limited step—toward that end? Why should we in this country want to give Peking ammunition to support its loud contention that "peaceful co-existence" as Moscow conceives it, is impossible?

Ever since 1959 we have told the world that we were prepared to stop test explosions in the atmosphere if the Soviets would agree. Can't you hear the ridicule and scorn that Mao Tse-tung would heap on the head of Khrushchev if we now reject our own proposal? I believe that the rejection of the test ban treaty would play squarely into the hands of the Chinese militarists and might lead either to the repudiation of peaceful co-existence by Mr. Khrushchev or to his replacement by a more militaristic Soviet leader. On the other hand, our acceptance of the treaty could very well have the effect of widening the split between Moscow and Peking.

We know that the dispute between Russia and China does not mean that our troubles with Moscow are over. The tensions between our two competing social systems will remain. We know that the Soviet Union seeks to outdo us in at least the economic and ideological sense of the term. But I do not fear peaceful competition with the Soviets. I have the faith to believe that our economy and our society and our democratic government are more than equal to that competition. I believe, too, that if we can avoid war, we will continue to see modifications in Soviet society and foreign policy that will improve the chances for a world of law rather than ruin. As the late John Foster Dulles said five years ago: "There is nothing inevitable about communism except that it, too, is bound to change. The forces that change it are already at work and discernible. Education that equips minds to find the ways to penetrate outer space also equips them to penetrate the fallacies of Marxism and its glittering slogans."

Merely in order to survive, the Russian leaders are constrained to recognize that they cannot force a communist mold on the world. They do not agree with our ideology, but they share our urgent desire for survival. Mr. Khrushchev and his colleagues are realists who must reckon not only with the nuclear power of the United States but with the concern of the Russian people. The ultimate hope of more peaceful relations with Moscow and indeed the hope for a more humane regime in the Kremlin depend in large part on our ability to discern and act upon those conditions where the interests of America and Russia coincide.

As President Kennedy said in his great speech of June 10 at American University:

Among the many traits the peoples of our two countries have in common, none is stronger than our mutual abhorrence of war. Almost unique among the major world powers, we have never been at war with each other. And no nation in the history of battle ever suffered more than the Soviet Union in the Second World War. At least 20 million lost their lives.

It is the Soviet Union and the United States that would be the centers of unspeakable horror in the event of another war. Likewise, it is these two great powers who are carrying the chief burdens of the arms race and who have the most to gain from a relaxation of tensions.

"We are both caught up in a vicious and dangerous cycle with suspicion on one side breeding suspicion on the other, and new weapons begetting counter-weapons," said the President. "In short, both the United States and its allies and the Soviet Union and its allies have a mutually deep interest in a just and genuine peace and in halting the arms race. Agreements to this end are in the interests of the Soviet Union as well as ours—and even the most hostile nations can be relied upon to accept and keep those treaty obligations, and only those treaty obligations, which are in their own interest." The treaty before us is in our interest and in the interest of the Soviets and the ninety-one nations that have signed it. The Chinese Communists and Fidel Castro do not think the treaty is in their interest, but fortunately neither of them is presently in a position to jeopardize its success.*

During World War Two we sang a song, "Praise the Lord and Pass the Ammunition." I appreciate the need for ammunition. It has at various times in history overcome tyranny and brought down bullies. But let us not forget that our nation has also come to greatness under a tradition of praising the Lord.

I see the banning of nuclear test explosions in God's heavens as an exercise in realism by earthbound men, but also as a hymn of praise to the Father of all mankind.

* The Chinese have since developed a nuclear capability.

■ *The easing of cold war pressures, highlighted by the approval of the limited nuclear test ban, increased hopes for a downward turn in the arms race. I was convinced that reductions in military spending would be approved more readily if plans were developed in advance to ease the transition from arms production to civilian needs; in the absence of such planning, I feared, painful economic dislocations would strike communities affected by cutbacks in arms output. Anxiety over such possible dislocations would manifest itself in opposition to reductions in arms spending even though such decreases were clearly indicated by any reasonable estimate of defense needs.*

To meet this problem, I introduced a comprehensive Senate bill, "The National Economic Conversion Act," providing for conversion planning arrangements to ease the shift from unneeded military spending to urgent civilian priorities. The legislation won the co-sponsorship of thirty-one other senators, strong editorial endorsement, and the support of many private groups in business, labor, industry, and elsewhere. For reasons that were never made clear, the Administration was cool, if not hostile, to the proposal. A small ad hoc study group was established by executive order of the President on December 21, 1963, to review problems presented by arms reductions, but this effort was given low priority and little came of it.

Interest in the need for developing conversion competence was stirred by a number of military-installation closings and contract terminations announced by the Pentagon in late 1963 and early 1964. Brief hearings on my bill, S. 2274, were held before the Senate Commerce Committee on May 25 and June 22, 1964. But the acceleration of the war in Vietnam gradually diverted attention from my proposal.

It is clear, nonetheless, that a society devoting over half of its public budget to military spending urgently needs to develop the kind of conversion capability envisioned by my National Economic Conversion Act. We have not done so.

Hopefully, the war in Vietnam will one day end; hopefully, we will then be able to divert part of our

swollen military budget to neglected needs in our cities,
farms, classrooms, hospitals, anti-pollution campaigns,
and other urgent priorities. I believe we should be mov-
ing now to enact the kind of conversion mechanisms
outlined in the presentation I made in the Senate in
1963 upon the introduction of my conversion bill.

The National
Economic
Conversion Act

This legislation—a bill to establish a National Economic Conversion Commission to develop plans for economic adjustments to changes or reductions in our defense expenditures—recognizes that the nation has found it necessary during the cold war years since World War Two to make a heavy economic commitment for defense. Our security requires a capacity to adjust our defense establishment to changing military and international conditions. Such a capacity includes preparation for the conversion of any part of our military plant to civilian purposes.

This legislation offers one means by which the people of the United States can safely embrace any reasonable future opportunities for converting the instruments of war to the tools of peace. It should add to the flexibility, the efficiency, and the strength of our entire security system.

Speech in the United States Senate, October 31, 1963.

Provisions of the Bill

A National Economic Conversion Commission would be established in the Executive Office of the President. The commission, headed by the Secretary of Commerce, would include the Secretaries of Defense, Agriculture, Labor, and Interior, the chairmen of the Atomic Energy Commission and the Council of Economic Advisers, and the directors of the Arms Control and Disarmament Agency and the National Aeronautics and Space Administration.

The commission would have responsibility for drafting a blueprint of appropriate actions by departments and agencies of the federal government to facilitate conversion. This should include preparation of schedules of possible private and public investment patterns resulting from various degrees of economic conversion, and the employment and income effects that may be expected therefrom. This analysis would be submitted to the President and to congress within one year after the enactment of the act.

The commission would convene, within the next twelve months, a National Conference on Industrial Conversion and Growth to focus nationwide attention on these problems and to encourage appropriate study and programming for economic conversion in all relevant parts of the nation's economy.

The commission would counsel with the governors of the states to encourage appropriate and timely preparation in support of conversion capability.

In addition to the National Economic Conversion Commission, the bill provides that defense plants under contract to the Department of Defense, the Atomic Energy Commission, or the Space Agency, shall have in their managements an operating conversion committee. Such committees would be required in all plants engaged in defense work for one year or more and whose personnel are 25 per cent or more so engaged.

Each industry committee would be charged with planning for the conversion of the facility from military to civilian work, as required in the event of contract changes owing to terminations, cutbacks, or stretchouts.

Many firms will find it possible to make appropriate plans for coping with conversion problems on their own, but others will be unable to plan with their own competence and will need the counsel and assistance of government.

Uncertainties of the Defense Economy

As the members of the Senate know, I have previously expressed the conviction that we have reached a point when we can make careful reductions in arms expenditures without in any way endangering the security of the nation. Regardless of whether this view prevails, we can anticipate a leveling off of numerous defense projects, and significant shifts in the character of defense spending. Plans to make economic adjustment to such changes should be prepared by both government and private industry. The bill I offer today establishes the machinery to inaugurate such planning.

Uncertainties, many of which depend upon factors beyond our control, provide the backdrop for the proposed legislation. The proposal is designed to ease the conversion or modification of our arms industries and installations to civilian purposes. If we are to avoid painful economic dislocations and loss of job opportunities resulting from reductions or changes in our defense system, we must develop procedures now for anticipating and meeting these problems.

The New York *Times* of July 12, 1963, reported that Defense Secretary McNamara foresees a "leveling off" of defense spending. As a result of cost-efficiency achievements, Mr. McNamara has indicated that annual savings of $4 billion may be reached by 1964. This does not necessarily mean a reduction in combat forces or overall military spending, but it does point up the changing character of defense operations. An earlier report, in the June 30 *Times,* indicated that administration officials are giving serious consideration to a substantial cut in the weapons-acquisition program of the Atomic Energy Commission. The Congress has recently reduced by more than a billion dollars the requested Defense Department appropriations for fiscal 1964.

The changing demands of our security in the 1960s necessarily involve a constantly shifting and changing defense establishment. For example, during the past two years, we have been allocating increased billions of dollars to our conventional-warfare and mobile-force capability. Simultaneously, we have been phasing out B-47 strategic bombers and modifying our missile system. Secretary McNamara has recently blocked construction of nuclear aircraft carriers.

These and other anticipated changes in defense allocations point up the uncertainty of any existing weapons system or military installation.

Even more fundamental changes may occur in our military forces and defense-related industries if the pattern of the cold war should shift substantially. There are new indications that Russia may be changing the direction of her cold war tactics. Mr. Khrushchev's disavowal of the moon race, his sharp differences with the Chinese communists, his expenditure of large sums for food, ought to be viewed with healthy skepticism, but they are indications, nonetheless, of a possible change in Soviet tactics.

It is possible that our rivalry with the Soviets may move more and more into an economic, cultural, and ideological conflict in which military weapons would serve an increasingly secondary role. If the President's hope for the test ban as "a first step" to peace is fulfilled by additional steps to peace, then surely we can anticipate a change in military spending by the great powers. Any significant success in the long effort to reach agreement on disarmament would, of course, sharply affect the level of defense spending.

In August, 1963, the monthly Survey of the Morgan Guaranty Trust Company reported that even though it might be premature to hope for a thaw in the cold war, the time has come to prepare for a reduction and shifts in defense spending. It commented:

Well before the Moscow [test ban] accord, a number of developments were suggesting the possibility of a break in the pattern of steadily increasing outlays for national security. Even clearer have been the signs that the composition of defense expenditure is likely to shift. Either event —reduction or restructuring—would impose economic adjustments on individuals, companies, and communities. The prospect, therefore, ought to be receiving consideration in the private sector of the economy, where adjustment would chiefly fall. Thus far, it appears to have been rather broadly neglected.

U.S. Economy During Conversion

Marxist critics of the United States have long contended that however burdensome, heavy arms spending is a necessary evil designed to prevent the collapse of U.S. capitalism. According to this view, were it not for booming defense industries and military forces to stimulate the economy and absorb our manpower, chronic depression would grip the nation. Many Americans, including industrialists, labor leaders, and public officials tend to accept this assumption.

I believe this to be a false view of the American economy. It is my conviction that with proper planning by both private and public officials on community, state, and federal levels, our economy can expand and prosper while undergoing substantial shifts or reductions in our defense establishment.

I agree with Minnesota's Senator Humphrey, who said in an address to the Senate more than a year ago [October 5, 1962] that "if we discuss the economic impact of disarmament on our economy, we shall reach the conclusion that not only is it possible to make such a conversion without serious dislocation, but it is possible to have a vastly improved economy, one in which economic expansion moves rapidly, and in which the production of goods and services increases for the common good."

In that spirit, I suggest the following propositions:

1. The United States clearly demonstrated at the end of World War Two that we could move quickly and successfully from a wartime to a peacetime economy at a time when a

much larger share of our total resources was devoted to armaments than is now the case.

2. Our present level of military spending—far from
strengthening the economy—is actually distorting and restrict-
ing the economy, weakening the competitive position of our
civilian industries in both domestic and international trade,
and seriously aggravating our balance of payments problem.

3. While our overall economy can absorb shifts in production patterns with comparative ease, certain industries, communities, and manpower groups would be seriously affected
by sudden shifts or cutbacks in the military system. These
special problems can be minimized with sufficient advance
planning.

During World War Two, U.S. defense expenditures
claimed over 40 per cent of our gross national product in contrast to 10 per cent today. Within a year of the war's end in
1945, we had reduced defense spending by 80 per cent. This
reduction represented three times the present percentage of
our national production devoted to defense expenditures. In
the same twelve-month postwar period, over 9 million servicemen were released from the armed forces—more than triple
our present total military personnel.

Despite this rapid demobilization and reduction of defense
spending, the economy boomed and unemployment remained
below 4 per cent. The satisfactory transfer to a civilian economy after 1945 was made possible partly because of the pent-
up demand for civilian goods and partly by our material
assistance to European recovery. It was also greatly assisted
by intelligent industry planning and government action, including tax reduction, veterans' benefits, concessions to industry, and a policy of monetary ease. All of these tested devices
could be readily employed again should major arms reduction
become feasible. Both the encouraging post-World War Two
experience and analysis of our present economic problems
point to the conclusion that a planned transfer to civilian
production can cause a boom, rather than a drag on our
economy.

Arms spending is not the unmixed economic blessing that

some citizens believe it to be. As William C. Foster, director of the Arms Control and Disarmament Agency, has said: "Defense spending of the type we now have has no intrinsic merit in terms of its ability to create production and income as compared to other forms of demand." A costly nuclear warhead resting in the arsenal is of slight benefit, if any, to the economy, whereas a similar investment in updated machine tools or classrooms or scholarships pays compound dividends.

Furthermore, arms spending is narrowly concentrated in a few giant corporations rather than being evenly spread across the nation.

Most disturbing of all, we are presently starving a number of crucial sectors of American society to keep the military animal well-fed. In recent years we have been allocating approximately three-fourths of our precious scientific and engineering talent to military research and development. This, plus the concentration of capital in arms production, has led to a painful decline in the modernization of our civilian industries. Many of our once top-rated civilian industries are losing their competitive edge both at home and abroad, with serious consequences to our balance of payments and our economic growth. The balance of payments problem is further aggravated by the cost of maintaining large numbers of American troops in Germany and by our military aid operations in Vietnam, Korea, and Formosa.

Even more difficult to measure is the loss to society from the diversion of much of our best brainpower—especially potential teachers—to military research and development. The shortage of talented, dynamic teachers and professors takes a heavy toll in American classrooms.

Every American should ponder the words of former President Eisenhower:

> The military establishment, not productive of itself, necessarily must feed on the energy, productivity, and brainpower of the country, and if it takes too much, our total strength declines.

Having contended that the arms budget is a restricted and sometimes damaging method of bolstering the economy, I nevertheless believe that it is so intertwined with the economic life of some of our communities, industries, and vocations that a military shift without advance planning would set off an understandable panic.

A significant factor in America's defense spending is its highly uneven distribution, geographically and industrially. Areas such as southern California, Boston, Seattle, Wichita, and a number of our states including Hawaii, Alaska, Georgia, New Mexico, and Utah, are heavily dependent on defense industries and installations.

In the aircraft industry, over 93 per cent of the employees are engaged in manufacturing war planes; in the shipbuilding industry, 60 per cent of the employees are involved in defense production; and in radio and communications equipment production, 38 per cent. These areas and industries, along with the technical personnel in related defense production, will be hardest hit by arms reduction or shifts in production patterns.

There is a wide range of American domestic needs that can easily absorb large public and private investment for new employment and economic growth. The nation's needs for resources development projects, particularly involving water, and for construction of schools, hospitals, mental health facilities, urban transit systems, outdoor recreation facilities, and rural development would more than absorb any likely reductions in defense spending.

There are many untapped opportunities in the civilian sector to which our defense industries might convert their capacity. For example, the airframe industry has competence for producing light-weight, high-strength structures useful for prefabricated housing. In the medical field, there are dramatic uses for electronic devices, to which part of our defense capacity could be diverted. Also, traffic signals in our cities could be controlled by computers to improve the control and flow of traffic. Countless other examples could be cited—and there are scores of ideas yet to be formulated for converting war production to civilian uses.

Scores of small communities have developed at the side of defense installations. We will have to make an imaginative effort to conserve the human and the capital resources of these satellite towns. For example, many bases include extensive facilities that could be converted into vocational schools and junior college use. The instructional staffs of some training bases are readily convertible into the teaching staffs of technical institutes. Indeed, such use of military training sites and personnel would help us to overcome at the junior college level the national shortage of technicians. This, in turn, can prove to be a major contribution to the technological renewal of many of our industries.

We should anticipate the possibility that a type and degree of specialization highly specific to military functions has developed in various occupations. Some electronics and missile engineers may discover that as specialists in aspects of missile guidance, there is no nearby civilian technology for which they are suited. For such men, there will be problems of retraining. This can be an opportunity for them and for our country. We all know that we must upgrade the function of educating our youth. Many of our defense industry experts could be attracted to the teaching profession with proper financial and professional incentives.

What is needed is a coordinated effort between private industry and government to smooth the transition. The bill that I have proposed will help to meet that need. Its combination of required industry conversion planning and state and federal supporting activity will help generate the confidence and direction needed for conversion capability.

With such a design, we will begin to relieve the concern that many feel, lest conversion from war production be the occasion of unreasonable hardship for Americans. In turn, the development of competence for conversion will make possible more realistic appraisals of defense spending, for then decisions on the termination of contracts or the closing of installations to meet legitimate efficiency and security requirements need not be blunted by concern for economic dislocation. This is bound to improve both the short- and long-term design and administration of our security policies. It will also add new force to disarmament discussions by removing fear of the economic consequences.

These proposed steps can help give our people a solid basis

for confidence in their own and our nation's future. With other related efforts, they can demonstrate that the best path to American prosperity and economic growth lies not in a constantly expanding arms race but in carefully gauged steps toward peace.

Reasons for Conversion Planning

There are various reasons why we must take steps to free ourselves from the fear of economic dislocation stemming from changes in our defense forces.

First, our military security requires that our defense planners be permitted a considerable degree of flexibility in weapons production and modification. As matters now stand, necessary changes or reductions in weapons systems or defense installations are often vigorously resisted by the affected communities and their political spokesmen. Such political and economic pressures, which freeze unneeded plants or installations into the defense establishment, weaken our overall strength. The Morgan Guaranty Survey observes, in connection with the inertia or resistance to change in defense expenditure patterns:

> With about one-tenth of gross national product devoted to military purposes year after year, there has developed a reluctance, both public and private, toward cutting back so sizeable a sector of economic activity. Thus, the very fact that makes it important to prepare for the possibility of a reduction in defense outlays—that is, the economy's heavy involvement in defense—could also make it more difficult to achieve reduction.

But in the absence of alternative plans, who can blame a community, or a labor leader, or a congressman, for vigorous opposition to the loss of a valuable payroll or dividend?

A second reason for planning conversion is that we have an obligation to protect our citizens in the armed forces and defense industries against an economic calamity. We need to replace uncertainty and anxiety with the assurance that conversion to civilian production can actually be a hopeful opportunity for the American people.

The senator from Pennsylvania [Joseph Clark], discussing the work of his Subcommittee on Employment and Manpower, has said:

> Certainly, it is a matter of direct congressional and national concern to inquire whether practical alternatives exist for the employment of defense industries and their work forces outside the defense program for the fulfillment of other community and individual needs . . .
>
> We cannot possibly leave great defense industries and millions of their workers in so vulnerable a position that they constitute an independent obstacle to the achievement of a stable peace. . . .

I want to clarify my purpose in introducing legislation at this time.

This is not a newly recognized issue, arising out of the apparent thaw in East–West relationships. The problem was recognized in the report on the economic and social consequences of disarmament made by the United States Arms Control and Disarmament Agency in March, 1962.

It was recognized by our colleague from Michigan, Senator Hart, in 1962, when he proposed a Senate Select Committee on the Economic Impact of National Defense, which was to study procurement policies and take into consideration the effect that termination or modification of procurement contracts would have on the economy.

It was recognized by the New York *Times* financial and business editors some weeks ago when they made a survey of conversion planning by our twenty-five major corporations that handle 50.8 per cent of all defense work. They reported on August 16, 1963, that "very little" planning for conversion has been done by industry, and that "many defense contractors simply refuse to consider a sizeable cutback in arms production as any kind of a possibility in the foreseeable future."

It was recognized by the Senate Foreign Relations Subcommittee on Disarmament in the study reported to us by Senator Humphrey on October 5 last year, to whose address I have referred.

We have been approaching the problem of conversion with increasing frequency and interest. We have some rather broad ideas about how it may be undertaken. It seems to the co-sponsors of this bill to establish a National Economic Conversion Commission that I have just introduced, that it is time to launch more specific planning for possible reductions or changes in our military programs.

The Anti-Ballistic Missile: a Security Delusion

While my proposal to reduce military spending received only two votes in 1963, I thought it might be one of those concepts, such as federal assistance to education, that appear less radical and more acceptable each year and are eventually adopted. The distortion of our society stemming from excessive arms spending seemed so obvious that I hoped we would soon see major reductions in military outlays and a common sense reordering of national budget priorities. I have believed for many years that excessive military spending weakens the nation by dissipating talent, brainpower, energy, and resources that are more urgently needed elsewhere in our national development.

Thus far, my hopes for arms reductions have not been justified. Since 1963, the size of our already incredible military establishment has grown enormously. Were it not for former Secretary of Defense Robert McNamara's opposition to many unwise weapons proposals, military spending would have increased even faster. Most congressmen are still reluctant to vote against an item carrying a "defense" label even though no rational case can be made for it. In the last year of his service even Secretary McNamara was unable to prevent the initiation of the most costly, wasteful, and transparently futile "defense" program of the decade—the anti-ballistic missile.

In order to appreciate the futility of the anti-ballistic missile system, one must first understand the technical issues.

A *simple offensive ballistic missile* is a rocket that travels into space and falls back to earth to its target. These missiles are made up of several sections, called stages, arranged with the largest at the bottom. On take-off the first stage usually consumes its fuel in about a minute. It is jettisoned and falls back; in turn, the next stages ignite, burn out, and are jettisoned; and by the time all but the final stage have served their purpose, the missile is well above the atmosphere and traveling at more than 12,000 miles per hour. The final warhead stage has no rockets of its own; it travels on its trajectory like a thrown stone. Shaped like an ice cream cone, or sometimes like a round-nose bullet, it is about six feet long and weighs between 500 and 1,000 pounds. It is usually built to hold a hydrogen (thermonuclear) bomb capable of wiping out a large city, but it could also contain devices for the dissemination of extremely poisonous chemicals or deadly disease agents.

The United States has more than 1,600 such missiles capable of reaching Russia; the USSR has about two-thirds that number capable of reaching the United States. Either force is enough to destroy any nation in the world several times over. Most of these missiles can be launched upon approximately one minute's notice.

It might seem that should Russia decide to attack the United States, or vice versa, it would make military sense for the attacker to destroy the victim's missiles before they could be launched and thus enable the attacker to aggress with relative impunity. Both sides have taken steps to eliminate this possibility. Most offensive land-based missiles are "hardened" —that is, they are buried deep in the ground in strong launching tubes, called silos, and are immune to anything less than a thermonuclear explosion directly on top of them or nearly so. Approximately one-third of our offensive missiles, and a smaller but growing number of the Soviet Union's, are carried in nuclear submarines cruising secret undersea courses off the shores of the potential enemy. These submarines can launch their missiles without surfacing, and they would be extremely difficult to detect and destroy.

Thus, each side has a "second-strike capability"—that is,

there is no doubt of either side's ability to absorb a full strike and still be able to retaliate with more than enough force to destroy any aggressor. As long as each side has the ability to destroy the other several times over, we are in a position of parity; and we will remain so regardless of how many additional missiles either side builds. If all-out war between the two major powers comes, it will make no difference who strikes first. Both will be destroyed.

This has been the situation for several years. Now a new device called the *anti-ballistic missile,* or *ABM,* is entering the picture. ABMs—short-range, high-acceleration missiles that can be launched on very short notice—are designed to intercept and destroy an incoming enemy offensive warhead. Because of the high speed of the offensive warhead and the short range of the ABM, it is not reasonable to expect a direct-hit interception or even anything we are used to thinking of as a near miss. An ABM is doing well if it can come within a mile or two of an incoming warhead; therefore, it is necessary to arm the ABM with its own nuclear or thermonuclear weapon.*

If an offensive warhead were to approach the United States, it could be detected by long-range radars while approximately 2,000 miles, or ten minutes, away from its target. By mid-1969, improved "over the horizon" radars will be in use that can detect offensive missiles almost as soon as they are launched, giving up to 25 minutes' warning. Various radars would follow the missile for a short time while computers analyzed its trajectory, predicted the path it would follow for the remainder of its flight, plotted an interception course for the Spartan anti-ballistic missile, launched Spartan when the warhead came within range, guided it into the path of the warhead, detonated Spartan's warhead at the instant of closest approach, and thus destroyed the offensive warhead

---

* A nuclear ("atomic") weapon operates by fission of uranium or plutonium. A thermonuclear weapon ("hydrogen" or "H" bomb), which is many times more powerful, uses a nuclear weapon to create the very high temperatures needed to initiate the fusion of hydrogen, from which it gets most of its power.

before it could re-enter the atmosphere. Since there is no air in space, there would be no blast effect; the offensive warhead would be destroyed by the intense radiation from the ABM detonation.

Spartan is a three-stage, solid-fuel rocket about 55 feet long and 3 feet in diameter that carries a medium-size thermonuclear warhead. Since it has a range of several hundred miles, it is estimated that less than twenty Spartan launching sites could provide an "umbrella" over the entire United States, whatever that might be worth. Unfortunately, it would be worth practically nothing.

A Spartan defense would be almost useless because it could not be in place before 1972 at the earliest. By that time the "simple" offensive warheads I have described will have been almost entirely replaced, in the arsenals of every country having offensive missiles, with more complex warheads incorporating various "penetration aids"—devices designed to enable the offensive warhead to penetrate an ABM defense. For example, a warhead could release a huge cloud of "chaff" —aluminum foil or millions of very fine copper wires which would reflect all radar beams. Instead of the warhead, the defensive radar would see only this large cloud. The defenders would know the warhead was somewhere in the cloud, but they wouldn't know where. Alternatively, the warhead could inflate and scatter hundreds of foil-covered balloons the same size and shape as the warhead itself so that radar would be unable to distinguish the target from the decoys.

Since this would occur in outer space where there is no air to slow down the chaff or the decoys, they would travel with the warhead. Once the warhead began to re-enter the atmosphere, of course, these light penetration aids would slow down or burn up and the warhead would again be distinguishable. However, by this time there would be only a few seconds remaining before the missile reached its target—not enough time for Spartan to launch and intercept.

To take care of those missiles that get past Spartan—as almost all of them would—we have developed a missile called *Sprint*. Sprint is a two-stage solid-fuel missile, about half the length of Spartan and carrying a smaller (nuclear rather than thermonuclear) warhead, but capable of such extremely high acceleration and speed that it can wait until an offensive warhead has entered the atmosphere and still have time to reach and destroy it. Unfortunately, the price Sprint pays for its high acceleration and speed is a short range, so short that it is useful only against warheads targeted within about fifteen miles of its base. Thus, it would be impractical to attempt to provide Sprint protection for the entire country. Sprints could only be used to give defense for specific points, such as population centers, industrial centers, or military installations.

"Thin" and "Heavy" ABM Systems

It has been the policy of the Eisenhower, Kennedy, and, until recently, the Johnson Administrations, that an ABM system would add nothing to our national security and therefore should not be built. In 1966 and 1967, however, we began to hear that the Russians were deploying an ABM system of sorts around Moscow. This stimulated various pressures, resulting in late 1967 in President Johnson's decision to approve deployment of a "thin" ABM system "for defense against a Chinese attack," which could be expanded into a heavier system if deemed advisable.

These are the components of the Administration-sponsored "thin" system:

1. *Over-the-horizon radar* would warn of enemy missiles almost as soon as they are launched. While this would be used by the ABM system, it is not strictly a part of it and will be set up regardless of whether or not we deploy the ABM.

2. *Perimeter acquisition radar (PAR)*, long-range radars and computers placed along the Canadian border, would track and analyze the trajectory of approaching offensive warheads.

3. *Spartan anti-ballistic missiles* will be scattered around the country to intercept small numbers of simple offensive warheads before they re-enter the atmosphere. Cost: $1 to $2 million each.

4. *Sprint anti-ballistic missiles* will be located at PAR and Spartan installations to defend unlaunched Spartans and associated equipment against offensive warheads that launched Spartans are unable to destroy. Cost: $1 to $2 million each.

5. *Missile-site radar (MSR)*, short-range radars, will be located at all ABM sites. Together with the PARs, MSR would guide Spartan and/or Sprint to the actual interception of the incoming warhead. Cost: $125 million each.

This system, called *Sentinel,* cannot be made operational until about 1972. The total cost of the system is estimated by the Department of Defense at $5 billion, but even the estimators admit it will cost 50 to 100 per cent more by the time it is built.

A heavier system, designed to reduce damage from a massive Soviet attack, is also under consideration. It would consist of the Sentinel system, plus the following:

1. *Multifunction array radar (MAR)*, a large and elaborate complex of radar and computers, is designed to evaluate large numbers of incoming objects, to attempt to distinguish the warheads from the decoys, and to decide which ABMs should be sent after which warheads. Cost: $400 million each.

2. *Tactical multifunction array radar (TACMAR)*. A small MAR. Cost: $250 million each.

Five to ten MARs and TACMARs would be distributed around the country.

3. *Additional Sprints and MSRs* at each MAR and TACMAR site, at each of our own offensive missile sites, and at various cities, to provide intensive defense for these points.

4. *Fallout shelters* for the populace of Sprint-defended cities. These are necessary because the Sprints themselves produce considerable radioactive fallout. Of course, if the local ABM system is less than 100 per cent effective—if a single offensive warhead gets through—the fallout shelters will be destroyed along with the rest of the city. Costs of fallout shelter systems being considered may run to $50 billion.

The Department of Defense has produced two suggested plans along this line. One, called "Posture A," would use

Sprints and MSRs at 25 cities—24 of our largest and most important population centers, plus the home town of the chairman of the House Armed Services Committee: Charleston, South Carolina, population 85,000. The other plan, called "Posture B," would include "Posture A" plus 25 additional cities. This "full" system, which would still leave 80 cities of over 100,000 population undefended except for Spartan, could not be made fully operational until 1975. It would cost at least $40 billion to build and $500 million annually to maintain. It is difficult to estimate the annual cost of improving the system and keeping it up to date since, as I will explain, it will be obsolete several years before it can be built.

I have consistently voted against funds for construction of any kind of ABM system, and barring unforeseen technological developments, I shall continue to do so. In my opinion, the ABM would in no way increase our national security; it would decrease it. It would be an incredible waste of money.

Let us consider the arguments used in support of the ABM, and the reasons for rejecting them. Some argue for a "thin" system only, which is the present position of the Administration. Others favor a heavy anti-Russian system, which is the current position of the Joint Chiefs of Staff.

ARGUMENT 1: We need an ABM system because the Russians have one. If they can prevent our offensive missiles from getting through, while we can do nothing about theirs, they will have the advantage over us and may try to wipe us out, or at least to "push us around."

REBUTTAL: They cannot prevent our missiles from getting through and they know it. Their ABM system consists of a ring of Spartan-type missiles around Moscow. That is all. Let us suppose for the sake of argument that they intend to build a very heavy ABM defense for all of Russia, although there is no evidence for this. It will take them years to develop and install such a system, but if they do so, they will find that they have wasted their money because our offensive missiles will have been modified with various combinations of penetration aids that will make any foreseeable terminal ABM system useless.

I have already mentioned anti-Spartan penetration aids involving "chaff" and/or balloons. Here are some others that will be effective against both Spartan and Sprint-type missiles:

1. Warheads can be equipped with steering rockets to change course at the last minute, making interception immensely more difficult.

2. Warheads can be equipped with or accompanied by transmitters to "jam" the various ABM radars.

3. Neutron-triggered warheads: Any nuclear or thermonuclear explosion emits an intense blast of neutrons. This is one of the principal means by which an ABM hopes to "kill" an offensive warhead. It is possible to equip an offensive warhead with an emergency trigger that will detonate the warhead when it receives a wave of neutrons indicating that an ABM warhead has just been exploded nearby. Even at the altitude of a Sprint interception, a large thermonuclear explosion will definitely cause damage to the people and structures beneath. Moreover, it will contribute to the blackout effect (see below). Whether the "trigger" can act before these same neutrons destroy the warhead (by melting critical parts) is not yet established, but it is a strong possibility.

4. Blackout: A nuclear or thermonuclear explosion creates a cloud of ionized gas lasting for several minutes, which bends and absorbs radar waves. The effectiveness of this cloud, which varies with altitude and size of explosion, frequency of radar beam used, and number of radars tracking a given warhead from different angles, is not entirely understood. Nevertheless, it is certain that during a massive attack, with the sky full of offensive and defensive explosions, the effectiveness of ABM radar would be seriously impaired if not destroyed altogether.

5. Saturation: The simplest and most effective penetration device is to simply send more warheads at a target than the target has ABMs with which to defend itself. If a city defended by twenty-five ABMs it attacked by twenty-six warheads, that city will not survive, regardless of how effective its ABMs are.

We are currently embarked on a program to insure that we can saturate any and all targets anywhere in the world.

Without adding to the number of our offensive missiles, during the next five years we will increase our number of offensive warheads from about 1,700 to about 7,000. We will do this by replacing the single warheads on each offensive missile with multiple smaller warheads. These warheads will separate during the middle part of the offensive missile's flight. In some cases, each will be directed toward a separate target; in many cases, they will have some of the penetration aids discussed above; in all cases, they will be far enough apart so that one ABM will not be able to damage more than one warhead.* Even if their system were 80 per cent successful, which is phenomenally optimistic, 1,400 of our warheads would get through. As far as the Russian people would be concerned, the difference between being hit by 1,400 or 7,000 warheads would certainly not be significant. It might not even be noticeable.

There is no danger of their defense temporarily outstripping our offense. An ABM system would take years to set up; our offense is so far ahead now that we will have no trouble keeping ahead no matter what they do.

It is said that because the Russians are building an ABM, *they* must think it necessary; therefore, it must be necessary for us. This is strange reasoning indeed. One might just as well argue that since Russia thinks communism is a good idea, it would be good for us.

Let us not invest the Soviet Union with mystical insight. They make major mistakes just as we do. They have set up a primitive defense, even less effective than our unreliable

* Incidentally, quite apart from the ABM question, these multiple small warheads will be capable of far more destruction than the single larger warhead formerly carried by the same missile. For example, the eminent physicist, Dr. Ralph Lapp, has calculated that 45 multiple-warhead, land-based missiles, carrying 3 to 6 warheads each, could strike effectively at 200 Soviet cities and 60 million people. Obviously, 45 single-warhead missiles could attack only 45 cities. While it is true that a large single warhead would make a bigger fireball and dig a deeper crater than a smaller unit of a multiple warhead, this difference would usually not be significant to the city under attack. Even the smallest unit of a multiple warhead is considerably more powerful than the Hiroshima and Nagasaki bombs.

system, that can give them no meaningful protection from our offensive missiles. We are expanding our offensive forces so that whatever expanded ABM system they build will be more than countered before it is built. Their recent offer to begin talks with us on missile limitation is evidence that they themselves are apparently beginning to realize that the money they have spent on defensive missiles has been wasted. Why should we copy their obvious mistake?

ARGUMENT 2: While an ABM system cannot stop a heavy Soviet attack, it can decrease the effectiveness of such an attack and thus save millions of American lives. (This argument is General Earle G. Wheeler's, who is chairman of the Joint Chiefs of Staff. Like some of the arguments to follow—as will be indicated—it was part of his testimony before a Senate committee in February, 1967).

REBUTTAL: So it could, if the Russians simply sat and watched us build up our ABMs without doing anything about it. Unfortunately, they will not cooperate. They will install multiple warheads and penetration aids almost as fast as we do. Their offense is almost as far ahead of our defense as our offense is ahead of their defense.

It is incredible to suggest, as some ABM supporters have done, that the Soviet Union would not want to spend the money to keep its offense ahead of our defense. I have no doubt that the other side believes that, if we ever become invulnerable to them while they remained vulnerable to us, we would attack them while we had the chance. They will not allow this situation to develop.

The Soviet Union now has less than 1,200 offensive warheads. By the mid-1970s, which is the earliest our heavy ABM system could be in place, it is difficult to estimate how many warheads the USSR would have, but 5,000 is probably a good working figure. Many of them will have penetration aids. Assuming that we actually build 5,000 ABMs, granting the most unlikely assumption that they will not be so unsportsmanlike as to attack the eighty major cities that will still be undefended, and assuming our ABMs to be 80 per cent effective, which they are not, this means that our country will be struck by 1,000 warheads.

Let us consider what these numbers mean to us as human beings. Congressman Craig Hosmer, a senior member of the Joint Committee on Atomic Energy and an enthusiastic advocate of the ABM system, has estimated the effect of an attack on the United States by eighteen large thermonuclear weapons:

> . . . Almost the entire States of Massachusetts, Rhode Island, and New Jersey burst into flames. So did New York City, Hartford, Philadelphia, Baltimore, and Washington, D.C. Essentially the entire East Coast from Portland, Maine, to Norfolk, Virgina, up to 150 miles inland, became one raging, all-consuming fire storm.
>
> At the same moment a 170-mile-wide, 22,500-square-mile circle of flame erupted across southern portions of Louisiana, Mississippi and Alabama from New Orleans and Baton Rouge through Biloxi to Mobile, destroying all within it. Detroit, Toledo, Cleveland, and half of Ohio met a single fate, as did portions of Wisconsin, Illinois and Indiana from Milwaukee through Chicago, on to Gary and South Bend.

He goes on to describe how Seattle-Portland, San Francisco, and 9 million southern Californians were incinerated. In the first few days 120 million Americans died.

Now let us see what Mr. Khrushchev had in mind when he said that after a nuclear war "the survivors would envy the dead." This is what the 80 million survivors would face:

1. Food stocks would be greatly decreased. Our national food transportation system would be destroyed. Much of our soil and water would be contaminated by radioactive particles.

2. Public health and sanitation would be disrupted, facilitating the spread of epidemic diseases.

3. Many of the survivors would be seriously wounded by the attack and urgently in need of medical attention.

4. Since physicians tend to live and work in population centers, they would be killed at a higher rate than the general population. There would be proportionately fewer doctors available. This would be even more true of specialists and specialized equipment.

5. In addition to its direct effects, radiation from the attack would greatly increase the rate of mutation of disease organisms. Certainly, some virulent strains would result that would be resistant to known treatment. Facilities for research, development, and production of new treatments would be almost nonexistent.

The interaction of all these factors would give the effect of "biological warfare" whether the attacker intended it or not.

All this from only *eighteen* warheads! Moreover, none of these hypothetical warheads carried the fatal new epidemic diseases the USSR has probably developed in its laboratories and installed in its missiles, some of which we know little about and with which we would be completely unprepared to cope.

This is why I am not impressed by the alleged ability of a heavy ABM system to protect us from all but a thousand warheads.

ARGUMENT 3: We need an ABM in order to increase the time in which we would be able to launch a second strike. The accuracy of Soviet offensive warheads—and thus the probability of their destroying our hardened offensive missiles if they caught them in the ground—is constantly improving. An ABM might ward off at least part of the first strike and improve our chances of launching our offensive missiles.

REBUTTAL: As I have pointed out, we would have at least ten minutes' and probably twenty minutes' warning in the event of a Soviet attack. Almost all of our land-based offensive missiles can be launched within one minute of the time of decision. If hundreds of offensive warheads were detected approaching our country, doubtless our commanders would launch a retaliatory strike immediately, without waiting for the incoming warheads to hit. Moreover, our submarine-based missiles would be unaffected by a Soviet first strike.

ARGUMENT 4: An ABM would "stabilize the nuclear balance." If the other side has an ABM while we do not, the situation is "unbalanced." If we both have ABM's, it is "balanced" (General Wheeler).

REBUTTAL: If the Soviets want to waste their money on an ABM, this will not change the essence of the nuclear "balance," which is that each side knows it can destroy the other.

If we feel compelled to waste our money because they are wasting theirs, we will enter a bizarre new cycle of the arms race. It is difficult to imagine a less balanced situation.

Competition is a part of the American tradition—generally, a good and healthy part. But when we spend billions to "beat the Russians" in all phases of the arms race and the space race, this is neither good nor healthy. When one asks why we must have an ABM system if it adds nothing to our national security, he may be answered, "America should be first in everything." This is an admirable sentiment, but it can well lead to America being first in those things that make headlines but mean little while we neglect those things that do not make headlines but mean a great deal.

America is first in the space race and first in the missile race, but we are not first in infant survival. There are twenty-three countries that have lower infant mortality rates than ours. We are not first in female life expectancy; we are fourteenth. We are not first in male life expectancy; we are twenty-sixth, and there are two communist countries ahead of us. Why?

ARGUMENT 5: We need an ABM to "inhibit Soviet leaders from concluding that the United States could not survive a Soviet first strike" (General Wheeler).

REBUTTAL: If for some improbable reason the Soviet leaders are not impressed by the real second-strike ability of our missile submarines and hardened launchers, why would they be impressed by an ABM system our own experts deride as ineffective?

ARGUMENT 6: A defensive missile system would "demonstrate to the Soviets and our allies that the United States is not first-strike minded . . ." (General Wheeler). The general also stated that we need such a system to keep Russia from thinking "that the United States would not pre-empt under any circumstances."

REBUTTAL: General Wheeler is arguing both sides of the fence here, saying that the ABM not only helps to convince the other side we might strike first; it also helps to convince the other side we *won't* strike first. But that is not the most important issue.

Whether the Soviets think we are first-strike minded or not, they have their offensive forces, which we and they know would completely destroy us if we were to attack them. It is this—not speculation on the state of our minds—that reassures them we will not attack.

And we should not want the United States to pre-empt (attack first) under any circumstances.

ARGUMENT 7: An American ABM would "continue to deny the Soviets an exploitable capability" (General Wheeler). Translated from the Pentagonese, this means that the ABM would "continue" to prevent the USSR from using its nuclear threat as a trump card in various confrontations around the world such as Berlin or Vietnam.

REBUTTAL: First of all, the Soviets appear to have an "exploitable capability" to the same extent that we do. But even aside from that, this argument has little validity. It is acknowledged by proponents and opponents of the ABM alike that both we and the Soviets can completely destroy each other, but neither side can prevent its own destruction, and that this situation will not change with the building of one or more defensive systems. Therefore, how could any ABM affect either side's "exploitable capability"?

ARGUMENT 8: Even if the ABM is useless militarily, it would be to our advantage to trick the Soviets into an expensive arms race because we can better afford it. This would dissipate their resources and weaken their economy.

REBUTTAL: Quite aside from the moral question of whether we should try to force a country into economic distress because we disagree with its government, it seems to me to be clearly against our national interest to attempt to weaken the Soviet economy. The Soviet Union has come a long way since the days of Stalin, both in domestic liberalization and in improved relations with the United States. Let us hope it will come a much longer way. All progress in these directions is inextricably tied in with economic prosperity. Like most people, Russians become more agreeable when their stomachs are full. To try to reverse this trend—to try to push Russia back into the economic and psychological state in which China is now—could not conceivably help us.

Beyond these considerations, the current fiscal and monetary problems facing us and the urgent needs of our own society are a vital argument against the notion that we can afford to squander resources on costly, unnecessary military hardware.

ARGUMENT 9: China does not have the ability to destroy the United States. However, by the mid-1970s she will have the power to destroy a few of our cities with a light missile attack. This could be used as a threat to get us to keep hands off in southeast Asia.

REBUTTAL: In my judgment, the more we keep our hands off southeast Asia, the more successful we will be in that area of the world. Be that as it may, here is why Argument 9 is invalid.

It is most unlikely that China, a country noted for shrewd caution in foreign affairs, would provoke its own complete destruction just for the satisfaction of killing a few million Americans. It is possible, however, that the Chinese leaders may come to believe that their huge population could survive the worst we could do to them and still have 200 or 300 million people left for the rebuilding. This is mistaken, especially if one takes into account our chemical and biological weapons, but governments do have an unfortunate tendency to believe their own propaganda if they use it often enough. It is a possibility, then, albeit a most unlikely one, that China might attempt such "nuclear blackmail."

If this is their intent, I do not see how we could stop them, ABM or no ABM. Should the Chinese become determined to sacrifice their nation for the satisfaction of hitting a few of our cities, there are cheaper and more reliable ways of doing it than with a ballistic missile. They could launch a low-altitude airborne missile from a submarine or disguised surface ship a few miles off our coast—an ABM would be useless against such an attack. They could equip a merchant ship with a large thermonuclear bomb, register it under a foreign flag, sail into New York, San Francisco, or any of our harbors, and destroy the port and the city; they could do this to all our major ports at once. They could even sail these ships into our ports and announce that they would blow up the ports unless we acceded to whatever ultimatum they were pushing at the moment.

Or they could send penetration-aided missiles against our major cities.

I suggest that we resign ourselves to the fact that China, like the Soviet Union, can cause us a great deal of trouble if it is willing to commit national suicide in the process, and that we must rely on its instinct of self-preservation not to do so. We have no other choice.

Meanwhile, I suggest that we can greatly increase our national security by lowering the level of international tension between us and the other nuclear powers, and by discouraging nations that have not already done so from becoming nuclear powers.

ARGUMENT 10: Suppose, through human or mechanical error, a Soviet missile were to be accidentally launched against us. Hopefully, the Soviet Premier would immediately contact our President on the hot line, explaining what had happened and offering apologies and reparations. Hopefully, as we saw that no further missiles were being launched, we would believe him, and war would be averted. However, there would still be that missile on its way to one of our cities. In this situation, an ABM could save the lives of millions of Americans.

REBUTTAL: This is the one situation in which an ABM would be useful, although since the Russian warhead would probably be equipped with penetration aids, we would need the $40 billion-plus system—that is, more than $40,000,000,000—rather than the "thin" system presently authorized, and we would have to hope that the warhead were not aimed at one of the eighty large cities without Sprint defense.

The problem is that this is a case of the medicine not being distinguishable from the disease. What if one of our own Sprints were to go off accidentally? Because Sprint can protect only within a fifteen-mile radius of its launching site, this means that Sprint complexes can never be very far from the city they are protecting, and that our largest population centers will have to have *nuclear-tipped Sprint missiles within the cities themselves.* Since the launching procedure for an ABM is entirely automated and lacks many of the safeguards and double-check procedures applied to offensive missiles, it is an interesting question whether we would be more in danger from an accidental Soviet launch or from an accidental launch or detonation of one of our own defensive missiles. I do not claim to know the answer.

In summary, there is no reason for us to build an ABM just because the Russians are building one. It would in no meaningful way reduce the ability of the Soviet Union to destroy us, nor would it eliminate China's ability to damage us. It would not increase our national security; it would decrease it.

The political history of the ABM is straightforward and disturbing. Throughout the early 1960s the Kennedy and Johnson Administrations took essentially the same position I have taken. The "military–industrial complex" advocated defensive missiles, but that was to be expected.

For years, the Administration successfully resisted the pressures from these sources. Then in 1966 and 1967 we learned that the Soviet Union was deploying primitive Spartan-type anti-ballistic missiles around Moscow. Here the ABM supporters had an issue they could take to the people: "The Russians have an anti-ballistic missile system and we don't!"

This could easily have become a major campaign issue in 1968. In a political campaign, it is far easier to make an accusation than to refute one. The accusation that the Johnson Administration had left us defenseless against Russian missiles would be perfectly suitable to a headline or a one-minute video news clip; the refutation would be, possibly, too long to hold the attention of many citizens. It was probably the prospect of this difficult situation rather than national security considerations that led the Johnson Administration to capitulate to the ABM pressures.

America's national interest is best served by avoiding war, particularly nuclear war. Nothing could be more "anti-American" than World War Three, no matter who starts it or for what reason. Our frightening deterrent power is helpful in making the idea of an attack on America seem irrational to any potential enemy, but wars have always been irrational and nations have had them anyway. We still have Americans who talk of "pre-emptive first strike" and of using nuclear weapons against Vietnam or Korea; we can be sure that their counterparts exist in the Soviet Union.

The best way to prevent war is to reduce the international tensions that produce it. The ABM, by setting off a new cycle of the arms race with massive military spending on both sides, is sure to shift the national mood in both countries toward greater hostility and away from reconciliation. We will be in serious danger of losing our most effective defense—the spirit of coexistence that has helped prevent any direct US–USSR confrontations since 1962.

At this writing, the indications that the Russians may be willing to go forward with discussions of nuclear arms limitations would seem to make it politically acceptable and clearly in our national interest to continue with ABM research and development but to delay production. This would give President Johnson's successor several years' time before the election pressures of 1972—time that should be used to inform and educate the public to the futility of the anti-ballistic missile.

An End to the Draft

Many Americans, grown accustomed to living with the military draft, accept it as a traditional, permanent, and necessary part of our democratic system. In fact, it is a relatively recent development—our first peacetime draft was in 1940—and it runs counter to an important quality in American life: the concept of personal freedom. Many of our ancestors came to this country to escape forced military service.

Public opinion surveys have indicated slightly over half of the American people favor continuing the present draft system. I have no doubt that, to a large degree, that attitide stems from the fact that the alternatives have too often been ignored or dismissed without careful study, leaving the impression that we have no other choice. Even the most prominent spokesmen for compulsory conscription do not regard it as ideal; they excuse it as a necessary evil. The Defense Department, for example, has supported the need for the draft law to maintain its military forces; but the Assistant Secretary of its Manpower and Reserve Affairs section says The Defense Department has "never regarded the draft as a preferred means of manning our military forces. Our policy has been that conscription is only justified if military manpower needs cannot be met on a completely voluntary basis."

More significantly, my own experiences as a college teacher, as a father of teen-age youngsters, and as a member of Congress, lead me to believe that a high percentage of those favoring the present system are too old or too young to be drafted, or sufficiently privileged to be exempt. There is a remarkable lack of enthusiasm for the draft among its prospective and current victims, regardless of their willingness to serve if called.

Small wonder. As matters now stand, millions of American youth are uncertain about their future because of the draft, an uncertainty needlessly imposed. Roughly five million men between the ages of nineteen and twenty-six are eligible —that is, they have not already served in the armed forces; they have not been rejected by the Defense Department on physical, mental, or moral grounds; and they do not qualify for hardship, educational, or occupational deferments or legal exemptions. Even with the Vietnam buildup, we draft only about one-tenth of their number each year, and in peacetime our needs are even less. Yet we force each of the five million to stand ready to take up arms in the event he falls among the ones who will be conscripted.

A young man has no way of knowing when he will be drafted, if at all. Many employers will not hire him so long as he is eligible, an understandable situation that is attested to by the Defense Department. One study indicates that 40 per cent of those in the twenty-two to twenty-five age bracket have been told by at least one prospective employer that they could not be hired because of their draft liability. If the employer is willing to take the risk, the individual is still faced with the possibility of an interrupted career or dislocation from advanced education.

Consequently, there is pressure upon the draftee to minimize his chances of being drafted—to rush into marriage, to remain in school, if he can afford it, even though his studies may not interest him, or to enter an occupation because it carries a deferment rather than because it is his personal choice.

Because of the Vietnam war, we have increased our military strength to some 3.5 million men, compared to a peacetime strength of about 2.6 million. Even if this level continues, only about one-half of our youth will be needed by the armed services at any time in their lives; yet the fate of all draft eligibles hangs on a strange series of variables, ranging from the idiosyncrasies of the local draft board to the availability of a college loan. Some are deferred as students, while others are sent to Vietnam within a few months of high school graduation. Many of the ones who are called consider it unfair, and many who are deferred are bothered by feelings of guilt or doubt.

And we should not overlook the fact that some of our most thoughtful youth have come to a genuine conviction that the war in Vietnam is a mistaken policy that is damaging the interests of the United States. Others regard it as an immoral or improper interference in the affairs of the Vietnamese people. For these young men, the draft is a source of torment that forces them to choose between participation in a war they sincerely oppose, a term in jail, or flight from the country. None of these alternatives can bring a healthy result for them or for the nation.

Spurred by the divisions accompanying our controversial foreign adventure, there is an unfortunate tendency on the part of many citizens to categorize these young people as fuzzy thinkers, draft dodgers, or worse. In most cases, that is an unfair indictment both of their motivation and of their convictions. In the years to come, we may be deprived of their enthusiasm, idealism, and ability because of a draft law that in their view forces them to commit crimes against conscience and humanity. Let us remember that following World War Two we prosecuted and convicted German military and civil officials for obeying their government rather than their consciences. No useful purpose can be served by ignoring the conscience and conviction of American youth.

I wonder how many of those who regard the draft as the natural order of things have asked themselves why this method of recruitment should be used for the armed forces when it is not used in staffing any other branch of government. Since the abolition of slavery, no private firm has been allowed to "draft" its employees; the government does not draft its secretaries and other civilian workers, though their total wage bill is comparable to that for military manpower. We do not draft policemen, though their work is similar to that of soldiers, and we do not induct astronauts, who face a greater risk of death. We do not draft teachers or physicians or nurses, although the need for them may be greater than for soldiers. Why, then, do we draft members of the armed forces?

Perhaps it is because we feel that all young men should be willing to serve and defend their country by bearing arms. But the draft certainly does not make young men willing to serve; it takes them, willing or not. Few people would contest the virtues of patriotism, but this still does not establish a fair method of determining which young men shall leave home and which shall stay home when not all are needed.

Perhaps it is because we believe that military service has sometimes helped to bring a more mature and responsible attitude to young men—in combination, of course, with the experience of the years that pass while they are in service. But, again, a voluntary system in place of the draft would not affect this. It would merely change the method of determining which youth will be exposed to those beneficial influences. The total number of servicemen would continue to be based on total manpower requirements, and not on the number of young people who may need external help and discipline in growing up.

A draftee is forced labor. When the army takes nineteen-year-old citizens who are earning, on the average, about $4,000 per year, and puts them to work for $2,000 per year, it may appear that the country is saving $2,000 per year per man. In fact, while the army is saving $2,000, the draftee is losing the same amount. Since both the army and the draftee are parts of the American economy, the country saves nothing. In effect, the draftee is paying an additional income tax of 50 per cent on top of his other taxes.

This is eminently unfair. We are not only asking him to donate his time and perhaps his life to his country; we are asking him to pay for the privilege! Since national defense is a service that benefits all American citizens, it seems only fair that all citizens should bear the financial burden of it, as they do of most other government services. If there is to be any inequity in this regard, it should be in favor of the service-man rather than against him. It is often charged that old men start wars and young men fight them; this may be unavoidable, but I see no reason why all of us should not share as equitably as possible in the costs of war.

Furthermore, it seems to me wrong that while some Americans risk their lives on the battlefield, a few turn extremely generous profits by supplying the weapons of war and by exerting political pressure for newer, bigger, and more expensive weapons. In an attempt to correct this situation, I have supported, and shall continue to support, an "excess profits tax," which provides that whenever our servicemen are engaged in battle, corporate profits above the normal level shall be returned to the treasury to help finance the war effort. I am not "anti-business" in any sense of the term, but I have yet to hear a convincing argument for the morality of war profiteering.

Correcting Inequities

A great deal of our current problem stems from the fact that modern warfare and defense do not seem any longer to require mass armies. There is considerable doubt whether we shall ever again need armed forces of the World War Two size; this means that a prime question is always who should serve in the army when not all are needed. Some would meet this problem by extending compulsion to all—assigning some to military service and some to other kinds of compulsory service. Such a system would appear, in many ways, to compound the problems we have already, and to be hardly consistent with the freedom of choice that we value so highly in our society.

Another of the solutions being discussed is a lottery system. This does have wide appeal among those discontented with the inequities of the present system. Under it, exemptions and deferments would be reduced to a minimum, and those of an appropriate age, say nineteen-year-olds, would have an equal chance of being selected. Thus, the armed forces would include some students destined for college and some high school dropouts, and, to the extent minimum health and mental requirements were met, equal proportions from all strata of society. It is argued that this system would eliminate the inequities we have currently, whereby our armed forces tend to include, among enlisted men, primarily the poorer and less educated, while college students and, until recently, graduate students as well, were "deferred." In many cases these deferments have extended past the age at which students would be subject to the draft; in any event, for a war of hopefully limited duration, deferment may be sufficient to permit avoidance of military service and certainty of service under combat conditions.

While eliminating some of these gross inequities, the lottery system would still suffer the same defects as the Selective Service System we have currently. Again, an undue burden would be put on the young; again, those who serve would incur a hidden tax of enormous proportions. We would suffer the same losses of efficiency consequent upon the drafting of men who may have superior contributions to make in civilian service and inferior contributions to make in military service. We would suffer the same loss incumbent upon the uncertainty of just who would be drafted, which prevents people from starting on useful careers until they know their number had been passed. There would be the same loss in repeated training of servicemen who refused to re-enlist for a poorly paying job not of their own choosing. We would have the same waste of resources in the armed forces because of failure to correctly count the cost of manpower.

Many observers have recommended patchwork remedies for the obvious biases for or against the rich, the poor, the well-educated, the ignorant, the black, the white. These well-meant remedies will not succeed because they skim over the root inequity—the forced impressment of a minority of our citizens.

The one equitable and efficient means for recruiting our armed forces, it becomes increasingly clear, is to do so on a volunteer basis. Such a system would be fully consistent with our best traditions and, remarkably, would avoid virtually all the pitfalls we have discussed thus far. Most of the objections to a volunteer system can be shown to be spurious or lacking in weight, and it has certain particular advantages.

An Army of Volunteers

One objection is that an all-volunteer army would be an all-black army, or that it would be an army largely composed of persons from the lower strata of society. There is first a question of fact. Blacks currently constitute about 9 per cent of the armed forces, compared with about 11 per cent of the nation's population. Blacks do make up a disproportionate share of combat forces—15 per cent—largely because their low socio-economic backgrounds make them less fit for more skilled branches of service, and because of their higher re-enlistment rate—45.1 per cent compared to 17.1 per cent for whites. But it is impossible for the army to become all black. There are approximately 1,700,000 black men between the ages of eighteen and twenty-six. Suppose all of these volunteer for the army, and suppose that the rejection rate among blacks continues at its current level of 50 per cent. This means that, even under these most unrealistic of assumptions, only 650,000 black men would be qualified for military service. If a reasonable size for a volunteer army is 2.65 million men, blacks could at most constitute only 24 per cent.

In part, the increasing technical sophistication of modern warfare may automatically keep the proportion of blacks and the poor relatively low. A modern army that needs persons with high technical skills would not hire the unskilled. If it were desired to maintain a given racial or social balance in the armed forces, this could be easily accomplished by refusing to hire volunteers after the "quotas" had been filled.

Finally, for those who are really concerned about the fate of the poor, and especially of the poor who are black, the volunteer army should appear attractive. It is an inescapable conclusion, recently supported by the Kerner report, that blacks are the victims of discrimination in civilian employment. The armed forces have been one of the few avenues open to the black by which he can improve his economic and social position; this is confirmed by blacks' high re-enlistment rate. Civilian opportunities should certainly be improved, and the availability of opportunity in the armed forces should not be used as an excuse to avoid increasing civilian opportunity. But mistreatment in the civilian economy should not be a reason to deny blacks the chances for economic and social advancement within the armed forces. If blacks and the poor generally are going to serve in the armed forces, they should at least be paid adequately for the job they are doing.

One argument against the volunteer concept that troubles me is the possibility that the public would decide that well-paying armed forces would be a sufficient solution to the critical problem of poverty and the associated problem of racial discrimination. We must not fall into the trap of concluding that the problem of making decent civilian jobs available for all willing and desirous of work is solved merely because adequately paying military jobs are available. The armed forces should be in a position of bidding for the services of young men who are part of a society that equips all for useful, remunerative civilian jobs and hence gives all a free choice between military and nonmilitary work.

It may be that we continue the draft because we are concerned about the quality of the men who would enlist under a voluntary system. It is a fact, however, that 49 per cent of our current armed forces are true volunteers: they were not drafted, nor did they enlist out of fear of the draft. In Defense Department parlance, they are not "reluctant volunteers." Our experience over the years has given no indication that volunteers are less capable, less brave, or less dedicated than conscripts. On the contrary, the experience of a career serviceman and the opportunity to train him more intensively are apt to improve his effectiveness.

Another danger that one may see in a voluntary army, one that troubles me deeply, relates to its very efficiency and the consequent possibility that our government will have at its disposal, at relatively little cost to the broad body politic, an instrument of potential danger as well as potential usefulness. I happen to believe that it is not desirable to have American armed forces act as world policemen, dispatched anywhere over the world to intervene in other peoples' affairs, however well-intentioned our interventions may be. One inhibition upon such intervention, no doubt greater than ever after our disastrous experience in Vietnam, is the reluctance we must all have to see our youth drafted into such expeditions against their will. But if, out of our large and able population, a small, efficient volunteer force can be obtained who for one reason or another is not loath to fight all over the world in other peoples' wars, may not this potential restraint on any unwise government leaders be lost?

This danger is one that I cannot fully exorcise. There is in principle a chance that out of a large population we may find a small class, happy to be paid for violence, who will lend themselves facilely to policies and acts in our name, which we will carelessly allow to be pursued because we are not personally involved. If this were to happen the world would be scarred and the good name and reputation and interests of the United States would suffer immeasurably. Our country's only brake against such a syndrome would be—in some measure as it is now—a vigorous and watchful civilian control over our military.

Probably the most usual objective to the idea of a volunteer army is that if we did not draft soldiers we could not get them to serve, but this argument hardly bears scrutiny. The peacetime draft is indeed new to this country, not having been instituted until 1940; until then our armed forces in peacetime had always been recruited on a voluntary basis. Indeed, with the exception of the Civil War, there was no recourse to the draft in any war until World War One. And contrary to some popular impression, the bulk of those actually serving in the Civil War were volunteers. The Civil War draft drew great opposition and little in the way of positive results. Hence, it is clear that it has been possible to man our armed forces without the draft through most of our history. And, it may be added, a number of other countries, particularly Britain and Canada, closest to us in outlook and political institutions, have generally and do currently maintain their armed forces without conscription.

A simple economic fact is that one can generally get enough of anything if one is willing to pay the price. The basic principles of our economic system indicate that a higher wage in any occupation will bring forth a greater supply of labor to that occupation.

The argument that there might not be enough soldiers without a draft then comes down to the proposition that there would not be enough soldiers without a draft, given the current wage and other remunerations offered to soldiers. If more volunteers were necessary than are forthcoming at the current salary scales, the salary scales would have to be raised. It might then be argued that the cost would be prohibitively high. But here we come to a central issue. If the cost is prohibitively high that means, simply, that the cost of the armed forces is truly prohibitively high and society is not ready to pay it. Conscription does not really make the armed forces cheaper. It merely puts the burden on the soldiers themselves by forcing them to serve for far less than it would cost to buy their services in a free market.

As we have seen, the average nineteen-year-old draftee pays about $2,000 per year for the privilege of serving—older draftees, who would be earning more at their civilian jobs, pay even more—but this cost appears nowhere in the budget. A voluntary system would require that the full manpower cost of the armed services be included in the Defense Department budget and appropriation, and that we face up to what our military establishment is costing us. A voluntary system would be more economical and more efficient than the draft for several reasons.

First, it would save on training costs. At present, more than 90 per cent of those who enter the services do not reenlist. This necessitates putting a man through expensive training procedures, receiving the benefit of his skills for one or two years, and then losing him. A new recruit must be trained to take his place. Not only is this procedure intrinsically costly, but it also means that a significant proportion of our most highly skilled military men, men who have chosen the armed forces as a career, must be tied up as instructors. Under a voluntary system, in which the average length of service would be considerably longer than the present two or three years, training expenses would be greatly reduced.

Second, an all-volunteer army would be less expensive because it could be smaller. The men would be more experienced and better motivated; hence, they would be more capable and efficient. Fewer of them would be needed and we would have a more effective fighting force.

Third, once the cost of military manpower is placed on the table, the military would be forced to use its people in a more efficient way than under the present system. No longer would we see a highly skilled individual capable of earning, for example, $10,000 a year in civilian life, doing menial or clerical work and being paid $2,000 per year, thus costing the individual $8,000, and depriving the country of $8,000 worth of productivity. If the services want a $10,000-a-year man, they would have to pay him $10,000 a year, and if they are going to pay a man $10,000, the people and the Congress will want to be sure that the nation is getting $10,000 worth of service.

It is argued by some, however, that a "mercenary army" could be dangerous. It is a fact of life that should our armed forces ever decide to take over our country by force, they could doubtless do so. It seems reasonable to think that draftees, who may think of themselves as civilians in uniform rather than as military men, would act as a brake on any potential military coup and as a force for the preservation of civilian supremacy in the United States.

This is an interesting theoretical point, but it may not be too significant. From the time of Napoleon to the recent tragic takeover of Greece, ambitious generals and colonels have been able to use conscripted armies to perform successful military coups, while Britain's voluntary system has had no noticeable adverse effects on her government. Under either system, the real power is in the hands of high-ranking career officers. Our safety lies in their continued acceptance of the American tradition of civilian supremacy.

Under either system, it might be wise to re-examine our military education and indoctrination programs. I suggest that we can best keep our democracy safe from militarism not by forcing unwilling young men into service, but by impressing upon all of our men in uniform that they are citizens of a democratic country first and servicemen second. Toward this end, I propose that better civilian control be established over all of our military educational institutions and training programs.

Proposals for Change

If the time has come for replacing compulsory conscription with a system of voluntary enlistments—and I, for one, am convinced that the time *has* come—then a number of careful steps must be thought out and acted upon. One issue of prime importance is the matter of pay.

Although numerous pay raises for the military have been passed since 1950, most of these have been not for first-term enlisted men but to induce officers and other enlisted men to remain in the armed forces. Nevertheless sheer justice would require that we pay men serving their country more than we now pay. The effect of the current pay rate is to penalize those who display their patriotism in this way; we should, therefore, immediately raise the pay of these men even if, for some reason, we thought the volunteer army were not feasible.

Such a step, which would be fully justified on grounds of equity, would also provide a test of the feasibility of the volunteer army. If the armed forces were to offer competitive pay and benefits, there would be little need to rely on the draft, and certainly not in peacetime. The effective recruitment programs already in operation would be given a tremendous boost if potential recruits could expect, as enlisted men, salaries, responsibilities, and opportunities for advancement commensurate with those they would find in civilian life.

However, that justice requires such an action is no guarantee that we will take the action. As long as the draft exists, there is little incentive for the armed forces to try to get wages for first-term enlisted men raised, and there is likewise little sentiment in Congress to raise these wages. It has been suggested, therefore, that Congress set a target date for eventual elimination of the draft. For practical reasons, the draft cannot, and probably should not, be abolished overnight; perhaps, too, the draft classification machinery should be retained for the unlikely event of another war like World War Two; but it must become stated policy of the government to eliminate conscription for peacetime or limited-war situations.

It might be well, once the draft is eliminated, to require an Act of Congress, rather than a mere executive decree, to reinstate it when manpower needs rise. It might also be well to tie future use of the draft to similar restrictions, such as higher taxes or rationing, on the civilian economy, in order to make very sure that the politically attractive option of levying the cost of the war on a small and uninfluential part of the population is foreclosed.

PART II

American Policy and the World's Trouble Spots

■ *Although 1963 was a year of improving Soviet–American relations, it was also a year when festering trouble spots elsewhere in the world—most notably Cuba, China, and Vietnam—challenged American policy. Of these three, it was Cuba that occupied the center of the stage for the period from 1960 through 1963.*

After a successful revolution brought Fidel Castro to power in Havana in 1959, relations between Washington and the new Cuban government rapidly deteriorated, culminating with the severing of diplomatic relations in the closing days of the Eisenhower Administration.

The flamboyant Cuban dictator had a remarkable capacity for irritating and frightening American officials and our citizenry. Thus, plans set in motion by the Eisenhower Administration for an invasion of Cuba by refugees with American assistance were carried forward by the Kennedy Administration—culminating in the disastrous Bay of Pigs fiasco in April, 1961.

The anger, frustration, and dismay stemming from this abortive effort further inflamed public opinion in the United States. Then came the potentially catastrophic Cuban missile crisis of October, 1962.

During all this time, an amazing portion of the time and energy of the State Department, the White House, the Congress, the press, and other agencies was fixed on Castro. It seemed to me that the preoccupation with little Cuba and her young, bearded dictator had reached a self-defeating level, where it was damaging our interests elsewhere in Latin America and around the globe. I was especially concerned for fear that the constant fulmination over Castro would divert our attention from the infinitely more significant purposes of the Alliance for Progress—a broad concept proposed in March, 1961, by President Kennedy, to lift the economy and society of Latin America.

As director of the Food for Peace Program, I had developed a special interest in Latin America after heading a mission there at the President's request in February, 1961. In an effort to put our concerns about Latin America and the world in better perspective, I devoted my maiden speech in the Senate to this theme.

Cuba

Last Friday Majority Leader Mike Mansfield warned against irresponsible discussion of American foreign policy and especially the Cuban question. The Senator from Montana expressed the view that "much of the discussion of Cuba by members of the Congress is not helping this nation; it is hurting it . . . We have indeed had discussions of Cuba, but discussion steeped in politics, panic, and the perversion of fact."

Recognizing that the late Republican senator from Michigan, Arthur Vandenberg, offered the nation a classic example of constructive bipartisanship during the critical years after World War Two, Mr. Mansfield quoted Senator Vandenberg's warning to the Senate: "Only in those instances in which the Senate can be sure of a complete command of all the essential information prerequisite to an intelligent decision, should it take the terrific chance of muddying the international waters by some sort of premature and ill-advised expressions of its advice to the Executive."

I have been reluctant to add my voice to the current clamor over Cuba and Castro. I wholeheartedly endorse the majority leader's warning that on this and other foreign policy issues, no senator should speak his mind until he has thought through the consequences of his words. But keeping in mind the counsel of Senator Vandenberg and the majority leader, I am constrained to speak out against what seems to me to be a dangerous Castro fixation that is not worthy of this great country. I submit that we have become so involved in charges and counter-charges about our Cuban policy that we have come

Speech in the United States Senate, March 15, 1963.

close to losing sight of the real interests of the nation in the hemisphere.

I have often wondered why the wily Khrushchev would invest so heavily in both capital and personnel in the kind of risky enterprise Fidel Castro is frantically trying to establish in Cuba. If his purpose was to enhance the influence of Castro and Castroism in the hemisphere, he must be bitterly disappointed with the results, for the Castro–Khrushchev embrace has had the opposite effect. By turning his revolution over to Moscow, Castro has sacrificed much of his appeal to revolutionary leaders and followers in other Latin American states. No thoughtful observer of Latin American affairs has failed to note the decline of Castro's influence in the hemisphere since his marriage to the Kremlin.

But if Mr. Khrushchev's purpose was to create in Castro a gadfly designed to divert the attention of the United States from the real dangers and challenges of Latin America, then he must indeed feel that his investment has paid off handsomely. For each day brings some mighty blast at Castro from a highly placed American politician or commentator.

Meanwhile, the real dangers to our security in the hemisphere—the economic, political, and social ills of Latin America —continue to fester. The United States has atomic bombs in its security arsenal, but on the side of insecurity we have a smoldering blockbuster on our doorstep to the south, which potentially makes Mr. Castro appear like a mouse trying to bring down an elephant. I refer to the 200 million people of Latin America who occupy a vast land, potentially rich and fruitful but actually beset by misery, sickness, injustice, illiteracy, malnutrition, and misrule. It is a continent cursed by a social system that concentrates enormous wealth in the hands of the few and consigns the many to lives of desperate poverty. But make no mistake about it, powerful social forces are stirring to the south of us. Latin America is in a state of ferment; it is, as one observer put it, "dynamite on our doorstep."

Neither Fidel Castro nor Nikita Khrushchev nor international communism is at the base of this explosive situation. They are the exploiters and the would-be beneficiaries of the tensions and illness that threaten the security of the hemisphere but they are not the fundamental factors. They are effects rather than causes.

Castro climbed to power over the carcass of a decadent political and social system—which he shrewdly exploited, but did not create. The appeal of Castroism and communism in other parts of the hemisphere springs from the same corruption and social injustice that paved the way for the collapse of Batista and the triumph of Castro. The real bombshells of Latin America are fused to the following conditions:

1. Two per cent of the people of the continent own more than half of all its wealth and land, while most of the balance of the people live in hopeless poverty.

2. Eighty per cent of the people dwell in miserable shacks or huts.

3. Illiteracy grips well over half the population.

4. More than 50 per cent of the people suffer from hunger and disease, and most of them will never in their lifetimes see a doctor, nurse, dentist, or pharmacist.

5. Most of the peasants live under primitive feudal conditions with no hope for land ownership, reasonable credit, or escape to a better life.

6. Several key countries depend on one-crop economies, afflicted by depressed commodity prices.

7. Most governments are weakened by unjust tax structures, excessive military budgets designed to keep the people under control, bad land ownership, and indifference to shocking social problems.

8. A population growth rate several times faster than the growth rate of production of goods and services exists in several Latin American countries.

Two years ago, at the request of the President, I led a Food for Peace Mission to Latin America, which took us to northeast Brazil. In this benighted section of the largest and most populous nation of Latin America our mission came face to face with the real challenge to the hemisphere. There we saw the wretched life of Brazil's 27 million peasants who are trying to survive in the feudal, drought-stricken sections of the northeast. There we saw the miserable mud huts, the total absence of sanitation facilities, the villages devoid of doctors, teachers, and adequate water and food. We saw, too, Fidel Castro's counterpart and alter-ego, Francisco Juliao, the flaming peasant leader, urging his wretched followers to seize the land and destroy the suppressors.

I ask the Senate to consider the real problems that confront us. Is it Juliao and Castro? Or is it the unstable, frightful conditions on which they thrive?

It may very well be that in the long view of history, the Castros and the Juliaos, for all their mischief and violence, will have indirectly performed some service in that they have forced us to give closer attention to our neighbors to the south. Likewise, they have confronted the ruling classes of Latin America with a stern choice between making long-overdue reforms or seeing themselves swept aside in a series of violent Castro-type revolutions. Sometimes the hand of Providence moves in strange ways. There can be no mistaking the fact that much of Castro's appeal to the oppressed rests on the knowledge that his presence has forced every government in the hemisphere to take a new and more searching look at the crying needs of the great masses of human beings. The real issue turns upon the question of whether or not the people can overturn an unjust social order through a peaceful, democratic revolution, or whether they will do it by a violent, communist-led upheaval.

The Alliance for Progress is a mutual effort to raise standards of living through the painstaking—often frustrating —method of democratic reform and economic development. The communists call for a quick upheaval that promises a new day through Marxist shortcuts, Castro-style; the Alliance for Progress will test the patience and toughness of all of us who believe in its promise. It does not appeal to the politician who wants a quick headline and a fast answer. It is easier to make loud speeches against an irritable, bearded dictator than to face the tough and sometimes painful tasks of making the Alliance for Progress work.

I suggest that we have had too many willing to shed the

blood of our soldiers in an invasion of Cuba, and not enough courageous and thoughtful men giving their attention to the real problems confronting the Alianza.

We have too many self-styled experts telling the President the inside dope from their private intelligence sources and not enough expert analysis of depressed commodity prices, rural credit problems, land reform, and population pressures. We have had too many post-mortems over the ill-conceived Bay of Pigs invasion—which might have damaged our standing in the hemisphere more if it had succeeded through American military intervention than it did as a miserable flop. We had no more legal right to undertake air cover or any other military aggression against Cuba than the Russians would have in invading Turkey. We have offensive nuclear weapons, not ninety miles from Russian territory, but in Turkey on the Soviet border, capable of pulverizing Russian cities in a matter of minutes.

The Cuban invasion, originally conceived in the previous Administration, was a tragic mistake both in conception and execution for which President Kennedy has bravely taken the blame. Why compound the error by probing the ruins of a mistaken venture and then calling for a repeat performance? I applaud President Kennedy's policy of wisdom and restraint since the Bay of Pigs fiasco. He has been firm and courageous in resisting the clamor of the warhawks. Last October he rejected the counsels of those who called for an immediate air strike against Cuba. He forced Khrushchev to back down, but he did it without war. He has since resisted those who have shouted for blood and battle and blockades.

Perhaps this is why for the first time the American people have indicated in a current Gallup poll that they have greater confidence in the capacity of the Democratic Administration to preserve peace than they do in the opposition spokesmen. In another recent Gallup poll, the American public registered its overwhelming opposition to an invasion of Cuba. The people understand better than some political figures that such an effort misses the real nature of the challenge before us.

The President put it this way: "I think the big dangers to Latin America . . . are the very difficult, and in some cases, desperate conditions in the countries themselves—unrelated to Cuba. . . ." The President has cited political and economic injustice, poor housing, illiteracy, and inadequate commodity prices as the big dangers to the security and well-being of the hemisphere. As the President has said, these are problems that must be faced and solved in the main by the people of Latin America. But he has also proclaimed our willingness to help. Hence, the hopeful and inspiring promise of the Alliance for Progress.

Hence, the Peace Corps units—which through the dedication and idealism of American youth are bringing new hope and pride to the villages of Latin America.

Hence, an expanded Food for Peace program—which among other accomplishments is now providing a nutritious meal daily to 8½ million Latin American school children and to 5½ million babies and pregnant mothers. Hence, the U.S. medical teams that are developing in Central America; hence, the growing exchange of students and teachers between the universities of North and South America. These are the tools of hope and life and strength with which America is fighting the truly significant battles of the hemisphere. This is our best answer to communism and Castroism.

It is not yet clear that the ruling groups of Latin America are aroused sufficiently to their responsibilities to make the Alliance succeed on a broad scale. Nor is it clear that we have grasped fully the nature and scope of the leadership demands that are upon us as a great and powerful nation. I earnestly hope that we will not dissipate our energies in a senseless fixation on Castro. Our mission is to point the way to a better life for the hemisphere and, indeed, for all mankind.

I conclude on this additional note, Mr. President: We dare not let our preoccupation with Mr. Castro and other irritants abroad blind us to our domestic responsibilities. If America is to fulfill its promise both at home and around the globe, we must move ahead on vital domestic fronts. We have a gigantic agricultural plant to be nurtured and stabilized; we are faced with the necessity of creating new job, educational, and recreational opportunities for our young people; our older citizens are confronted by rising medical and hospital costs; we need to consider seriously the relationship of our tax and fiscal policies to a sluggish national economy—these and many other mounting challenges call for clear minds and steadfast spirits. It is no longer possible to separate America's domestic health from our position in world affairs.

Let us then move forward with a courage and prudence commensurate with our traditions and our responsibility as a great nation.

■ *For many years prior to service in the Senate, I had believed that our policy toward mainland China was narrowly drawn and self-defeating. As a graduate student in history at Northwestern University during the late 1940s, it seemed to me that it was not in our national interest to intervene in the Chinese civil war then raging between the Chiang Kai-shek government and the rebel forces under Mao Tse-tung. The billions of dollars in arms and aid that we were pouring into China in the absence of needed steps against corruption and injustice on the part of the ruling Chiang regime seemed to me a case of throwing good money and prestige after bad.*

In spite of our aid, the Chinese government collapsed in 1949 before the Maoist challenge, and Chiang fled to the Island of Formosa to establish a government in exile—which we recognized as the legitimate government of mainland China. Thus began the policy that we have followed for two decades: a policy of isolating and boycotting the Chinese mainland, while recognizing and generously aiding the forces of Chiang on Formosa. This course deprived us of the kind of interchange with the world's largest nation that was urgently needed to lessen the misunderstanding, hostility, and fear that existed between the two countries.

My public statements as a graduate student and college teacher in the late 1940s and early 1950s, recommending that instead of turning our backs on China we try to draw her into a more normal relationship with ourselves and the world community, became the basis of a heated issue in my first bid for the U.S. House of Representatives in 1956. The voters of South Dakota supported me in that campaign, however, which helped to convince me that public opinion on the China issue has been far in advance of the State Department and the Congress.

It was the recollection of this earlier encounter with the *question of American policy toward China that helped give me the incentive to speak on this subject on the Senate floor.*

China

"We must change to master change."

This little-noted phrase from President Lyndon Johnson's State of the Union Message of January 12, 1966, deserves a place in American state papers comparable to Franklin Roosevelt's "We have nothing to fear . . ." John Kennedy's "Ask not what your country can do for you . . ." and Dwight Eisenhower's warning of the growing "military–industrial complex."

Significantly, President Johnson advanced this concept in relation to domestic concerns—his plea for a "Great Society." The President was not, of course, calling for change merely for the sake of change; rather, he was suggesting that new challenges require new responses. Experiences as a youth growing up under difficult circumstances and long years in public life have led our President to reject the easy slogans that too many of us have accepted until recently. Notions such as "the unemployed are too lazy to work"—"the Negro should stay in his place"—"old people who have not saved up for a rainy day deserve the poorhouse"—and other once-accepted platitudes no longer serve the needs of a growing America.

In the enigmatic field of foreign policy, however, we have been slow to break free from the tyranny of slogans. While a changing world cries out for recognition that "we must change to master change," we are still guided in some areas by notions that have little relevance to present realities. If we are to avoid unrealistic crusades abroad that dissipate our moral and material strength, we must begin to apply the imaginative, up-to-date approaches to foreign policy that our President has brought to domestic concerns.

Nowhere has our failure to adapt policy to change been

Speech in the United States Senate, May 3, 1966.

more apparent than in Asia—especially in China and Vietnam. If our painful and frustrating involvement in the Vietnamese conflict has finally triggered an examination of American policy in Asia, this could represent the one positive result from an otherwise melancholy venture. As one who questions some of the assumptions that have sent so many American troops to war in southeast Asia, I believe that a fundamental reappraisal of policy is vital to our security as well as to the peace of the world.

Yet the most powerful forces moving in Asia since 1945 have not been communism, but nationalism and the "revolution of rising expectations." With the collapse of the old British, French, Dutch, and Japanese imperial systems during and after World War Two, Asia was convulsed by revolutionary forces aimed at throwing off outside control and securing a better life for the people.

Our own revolutionary, democratic tradition enabled some Americans to understand these fundamental forces. Believing that imperialism had run its course by the end of World War Two, our government encouraged the British to liquidate their Asiatic colonial system; we insisted that Japan surrender her imperial holdings; we brought considerable pressure on the Dutch to withdraw from the East Indies; and we granted full independence to the Philippines.

But in China and Vietnam, the revolutionary leaders were communists, which automatically made them the enemy in American eyes. To our policymakers, especially after the bitter experience of the Korean War, Mao Tse-tung and Ho Chi Minh were part of a worldwide communist monolith bent upon global conquest. We seemed ready to ostracize any communist government no matter how strong its base of local support, and to embrace any ally no matter how odious and ineffective, provided he carried an anticommunist banner. Having substituted communism for the devil, we felt sufficiently free from sin to rebuke those who failed to enlist on the side of right. Although we had followed a policy of avoiding involvement in European alliances of the nineteenth century, Secretary of State Dulles regarded neutralism as "immoral" when practiced by the newly emerging governments of the post-World War Two period. Forgetting that what we are *for* has been the source of our strength more than what we are *against*, we made anticommunism the guiding principle of our policy in Asia.

Thus, although Ho Chi Minh had stood with us in the war against Japan and saved American pilots shot down over the jungle, we backed the French effort to crush the Vietnamese independence struggle led by Ho. This action ran counter to President Franklin Roosevelt's view that Indochina should be placed under a UN trusteeship and prepared for independence. "France has milked it for one hundred years," Roosevelt said; "the people of Indochina are entitled to something better than that." But with his death, that view faded and $2 billion in American aid went to the French effort that ended in defeat at Dien Bien Phu in 1954.

Ho Chi Minh emerged as a victorious hero from the eight-year war against France—not because he was a communist, but because he tapped powerful forces of nationalism and popular revolution as a counter to a crumbling colonialism and an inept puppet regime. The evidence is convincing that if we had accepted Ho and permitted the Vietnamese to work out their affairs free from U.S. involvement, North and South Vietnam would have united under Ho. Such a regime might have served as a more effective buffer to Chinese penetration of southeast Asia than the divided and warring two Vietnams we helped initiate, which have been the occasion for so much grief over the past decade.

However lofty our motives, Americans in Vietnam and the various political chiefs we have embraced in Saigon since 1954 have suffered from many of the same handicaps that plagued the French. In spite of enormous outlays of U.S. financial and military aid, it has been seemingly impossible to establish a government in South Vietnam capable of enlisting a dependable popular counterforce to the followers of Ho. Perhaps no one of the dozen regimes that have come and gone in Saigon in recent years could have stood without powerful U.S. props. Yet, the public embrace of a white western power has also raised serious problems for the fleeting governments in Saigon, as General Ky has discovered in the Buddhist demonstrations.

Given the current nationalistic sentiment of Asia, an American military embrace of the local politicians may embarrass and weaken them, while undercutting our own position. In Indonesia, for example, it was only after the American presence was diminished that local anticommunist groups, freed from the charge that they were American stooges, took over and administered a severe setback to the pro-Chinese communist forces.

We have supposed that the number one enemy of Asia was communism and that any sacrifice to contain it would be popular. But few Asiatics share our obsession with communism. The bad memories that fester in Asian minds are associated not with communism, but with western imperialism and corrupt local hierarchies. The exploitative capitalism Asiatics have experienced bears little resemblance to the enlightened economy and public policies that have served America so well. So, while anticommunism has been an effective rallying cry to secure ever larger congressional authorizations of American military and financial aid for complaint regimes in Saigon and elsewhere, it has not been in tune with the strongest aspirations of the people of Asia. Too often we have become identified with corrupt, stupid, and ineffective dictators who made the communist revolutionists look appealing by comparison.

The obsession with communism that pulled us into the Vietnamese struggle has even more clearly dictated our policy toward China for the past two decades. In spite of the enormous power of the United States and the relative weakness of China, anticommunism has been a blinding light that has led us to aggravate the very dangers we most ought to diminish—the increased belligerence of China—the disruption of normal communications—a growing military involvement on China's border that could ignite a third world war.

Considering our sacrifices in World War Two to save China from the Japanese, we were disappointed and alarmed by the collapse of Chiang Kai-shek before the communist forces of Mao Tse-tung. This was an especially painful experience for Americans because we had prided ourselves on the "open door policy," our use of the Boxer Rebellion indemnities to finance Chinese students studying in the United States, our Christian missionary activity, and the Pacific war of the 1940s.

Americans blamed each other for "losing China"—forgetting that China was not ours to lose. Many Americans saw Chiang Kai-shek as a Christian statesman allied through his charming wife with the wealthy Soong family, devoted to justice and freedom. Actually, Chiang and the Soongs presided over a corrupt regime with little concern for the ordinary citizen. They mulcted both the U.S. aid program and their own people, while ruthlessly suppressing their critics. It was such a regime that paved the way for a communist triumph.

The galling presence of a communist government over the most populous nation on earth—especially a nation toward which we felt a peculiar paternalism—helps to explain why we almost literally closed our eyes to Chinese realities after 1949.

Instead of quickly recognizing the fact of Mao's government in Peking, we assisted the flight of Chiang to the Island of Formosa and set him up as the recognized government of the nation that had just expelled him. There was some discussion in U.S. circles about recognizing the government in Peking, but such talk ended with the eruption of "McCarthyism" and the strident anticommunism of the early 1950s. A well-financed "China lobby" skillfully cultivated American political, religious, and military circles to secure maximum aid for Chiang and implacable opposition to the new government on the mainland.

Thus was forged United States policy toward mainland China—a policy based on the political, economic, diplomatic, and psychological isolation of China combined with a bristling military containment. We have stoutly refused to recognize Peking and have blocked her entrance to the United Nations while insisting that Chiang's forces on the Island of Formosa constitute the real Chinese government. No American trade has been permitted with mainland China, and we have tried strenuously to discourage other nations from trading with her. Travel by U.S. citizens, first-hand observation, study and reporting by our scholars and journalists, the exchange of scientific, cultural, and entertainment personalities and works—all of these have been obviated by our non-recognition policy as well as by the bitter anti-Americanism of Peking.

The "Ignorance Curtain"

If an "iron curtain" describes the barriers that separated the Soviet Union from the West in the postwar years, an "ignorance curtain" has descended between the United States and China since 1949. American ignorance of conditions in China is paralleled by even greater ignorance in China of the American people—of our concerns, our aspirations, our motives—although their leaders make certain that our faults are well-advertised. The lack of information and understanding based on normal exchanges is one of the most serious by-products of the U.S.–China estrangement. Says China expert Doak Barnett: "There is less responsible public discussion in the United States of China policy than of any other foreign policy question of comparable importance." The meagerness of responsible public discussion is accented by the scarcity of competent China experts and researchers. Within the State Department, the McCarthy witchhunts of the 1950s took a heavy toll of competent, forthright specialists. Since then, State Department authorities have been largely muzzled by their fears of Congress while Congress has been muzzled by fears of the American public. The result is a paralysis of policy and a continuing ignorance that denies policymakers, the Congress, and our citizenry the opportunity to consider realistic alternatives.

The progression of the recent Senate Foreign Relations Committee hearings from the Vietnam issue to China policy has at long last focused public attention on the challenge of China. This may prove to be the most valuable service of Senator Fulbright and his committee.

In a complex policy area isolated for so many years from searching investigation and discussion, it will be difficult to devise acceptable new alternatives. No one of us has the competence to move with certainty in this long-shrouded field.

But our national interest as well as the peace of mankind demand that we open the curtain of ignorance with searching questions, even if the answers are not immediately clear. We need to ask whether it serves American security or world peace for us to ignore a nation that embraces a quarter of the world's people. Even if one assumes that the Chinese are trying to stab us in the back, the most dangerous stance would be to turn our back.

It may be contended, as has Secretary of State Rusk, that the Chinese have done much to isolate themselves. But does it really serve our interests to encourage Chinese isolationism through official American policy? Would it not make more sense from our point of view to revive the "open door"? Do communist states evolve in a more moderate direction when they are deprived of diplomatic, cultural and economic relationships with the community of nations? One wonders if nations, like individuals, do not become more hostile when they are ostracized by the community.

History and elementary psychology would seem to point us toward policies designed to bring China into the family of man rather than to exclude her. For sixteen years prior to 1933 we refused to recognize the Soviet Union. Since 1933 our relations with the Soviets have not been easy, but neither have they been entirely bad. We fought a great war as allies with the Russians from 1941–45—a war that might have resulted in the triumph of Hitler over western civilization had it not been for the enormous sacrifices of the Russian people. We have had many irritations and frustrations in our relations with the Soviets, but is there any responsible person who believes that Russia would have behaved more reasonably if she had been excluded from the United Nations, denied diplomatic recognition by the United States, and isolated economically and culturally from the west? The evidence is convincing that Russia's relationships with us and other nations have encouraged her more responsible position in world affairs. Soviet vetoes and speeches have often irritated us, but who would deny the beneficial impact of bringing Moscow under the subtle discipline of the United Nations family? Furthermore, as they have strengthened their own economy and society, the Russians have become less belligerent and ideological —more moderate and pragmatic. This seems to be the historical pattern of revolutionary societies, and may very well be true of the Chinese revolution.

It is never easy to forecast the course of history, but of one fact we can be certain—men and nations change with the years. Today's enemies become tomorrow's allies. As Justice Holmes observed, "Time has upset many fighting faiths . . ." History provides grounds for hope that the militant passions that now divide China and the United States may come into more balanced proportion with the passing of time. The Holy Crusades of the Middle Ages once enlisted the deepest emotions of Christians against the Moslems. But a modern authority, Sir Steven Runciman, looking back on this period, writes: "The triumphs of the Crusades were the triumphs of faith. But faith without wisdom is a dangerous thing . . . There was so much courage and so little honor, so much devotion and so little understanding. High ideals were besmirched by cruelty and greed, enterprise and endurance by a blind and narrow self-righteousness; and the Holy War itself was nothing more than a long act of intolerance in the name of God, which is the chief sin against the Holy Ghost."

The lesson of the Crusades would seem to counsel, not another Holy War, but patience and restraint on our part while time works its way in the relations between China and the United States.

It may be argued that China is too aggressive to warrant membership in the international community. The growing bitterness between Russia and China might even lead the Russians to this view. There have been many belligerent, fanatical pronouncements from Peking; and no one can fully comprehend Chinese behavior. Both Moscow and Washington are vilified daily—the United States is denounced alternately as a "paper tiger" and as an aggressor bent upon destroying China with the connivance of Moscow. Sino–Soviet expert Professor Donald S. Zagoria has noted that the Chinese bitterness toward Russia, whom they regard as a traitor, is more intense than their feeling about the United States, whom they view simply as an enemy.

In any event, the gap between Chinese rhetoric and actual aggression is sufficiently wide to indicate that their bellicose utterances may be born more of fear and damaged pride than of any serious intent or capacity to conquer the world. The recent highly publicized document by Marshal Lin Piao—far from being a Chinese *Mein Kampf*—actually seems to be a warning to China's friends in Vietnam and elsewhere that they must fight their wars of liberation with little or no help from China. In fact, Peking has been restrained and cautious in committing its military power abroad. Even in the Korean War, the Chinese did not enter until they saw American troops approaching their frontier after warnings that they would not tolerate this development; while sending "volunteers" into Korea, the Chinese refrained from the use of airpower. In the 1962 border conflict with India, the claims of Peking were fully supported by the Nationalist Chinese government on Formosa and by some informed people in neutral states; when the Chinese armies pushed easily beyond the disputed area, they were quickly withdrawn to the line claimed by Peking as the legitimate boundary.

It is, of course, true that Peking is giving limited aid to North Vietnam and the Viet Cong in the current Vietnamese war. But so far no Chinese soldiers are fighting in South Vietnam nor has Chinese airpower appeared, in spite of heavy and persistent American attacks close to the Chinese border.

At home, China is beset with enormous problems of too little food, too many people, and incredible difficulties of organization and development. She lacks the economic base, the food supply, the navy, and the airpower to protect herself, to say nothing of waging a major war abroad.

None of this excuses China's belligerence—for example, her brutality in Tibet. It does, however, suggest that there is a considerable gap between the fire-eating pronouncements of the Chinese and their inclination or capacity to engage in overt aggression.

It should not be difficult to imagine that China is genuinely fearful of her present posture. She sees her former ally, the Soviet Union, moving into a cooperative relationship with the west. She sees the mighty American Seventh Fleet maneu-

vering constantly off her shores and fast-flying American
planes bombing daily close to her frontiers. She sees Chiang—
with his 600,000-man army and air force backed by the United
States—still insisting that he will return to the mainland. She
sees herself ringed by American nuclear installations capable
of pulverizing her cities. Heavily loaded U.S. bombers are
poised on bases in Formosa, Okinawa, Japan, the Philippines,
Thailand, and South Vietnam. Remembering our frightened
and angry reaction to the installation of Russian missiles in
Cuba in 1962, it should not be difficult for us to understand
China's reaction to the ring of U.S. nuclear power that con-
fronts her. What would be our attitude if enormous Chinese
air power were pointed at us from bases in Mexico City, Mon-
treal, Staten Island, and Bermuda?

This kind of "containment" invokes painful Chinese
memories of a century of humiliation and exploitation at the
hands of the western powers. Beginning with the Opium Wars
of the 1840s the European states, including Czarist Russia,
ruthlessly carved out areas of exploitation in China that were
sealed with "the unequal treaties." This experience was especially traumatic for the Chinese because of their deeply rooted
sense of cultural superiority. "This humiliation," writes China
observer Charles Taylor, "still deeply felt, helps to explain the
curious mixture of concern and defiance with which China
regards the military power now ranged around its borders."

The triumph of the communists in 1949 ended western
exploitation, but Chinese leaders bear the scars not only of a
century of shame; they especially recall America's effort in the
recent past to crush them in their struggle with Chiang Kai-
shek. Now they see their country surrounded by massive American power while their former ally, the Soviet Union, has
apparently deserted them. Chinese foreign policy is aimed at
the diminution of U.S. military power in Asia, the annexation
of China's former territories—especially Formosa—and the
acceptance of China as a great power. In effect, China would
like to establish a Monroe Doctrine that would give her the
kind of role in Asia that we proclaimed for ourselves in the
western hemisphere. The Chinese mistakenly expected the
Russians to back up their objectives much as the British fleet

supported the Monroe Doctrine for us during the nineteenth century.

Peking's current goals would doubtless be pursued by any strong Chinese government—communist or noncommunist. The evidence is compelling, however, that China will not recklessly commit her military power. But even if one accepts Chinese belligerence at face value—even if China has done much to isolate herself, and even if she repeatedly spurns U.S. initiatives toward improved relations—I believe that American policy should now be pointed toward achieving a reconciliation with the people and the government of this vast country. The United States is great enough and powerful enough and wise enough to take the lead during the next decade or two in modifying the bitterness and fear that have developed between China and ourselves.

1. A first step in that direction should be a careful examination—accompanied by public discussion—of all aspects of our China policy.

There is no more urgent responsibility confronting American scholars, journalists, members of Congress, and government officials than a re-examination and restructuring of Sino–American relations. A problem so important to ourselves, our children, and all mankind should be analyzed and discussed with candor and with courage. Senator Fulbright has helped to set us on that course by the stimulating investigation recently conducted by his committee. The discussions launched by the Senate Foreign Relations Committee should be broadened and pursued in depth. To strengthen that effort, I would suggest that the President name a blue-ribbon China commission of highly qualified Americans, headed perhaps by former President Eisenhower or Generals Ridgway or Gavin. Such a commission could look carefully at the various aspects of U.S.–China relations and recommend needed policy changes or initiatives.

A distinguished commission of this kind would have the authority and prestige to marshal the finest talent in the nation and make their views known to the American people. Qualified men specializing in China are sadly lacking in the State Department, although there are a handful of highly able experts there as well as in some of our great universities. But such brilliant men as George Kennan, Charles Bohlen, and Llewellyn Thompson—experts on Soviet affairs—are not easily found in the China section of the State Department. We need to be about the business of developing such men and harnessing their talent as quickly as possible.

2. China should be invited to participate in the disarmament and nuclear proliferation talks at Geneva. This suggestion, advocated by Senator Robert Kennedy and others, is clearly in our national interest. If we believe that China is a potentially dangerous nuclear power, it makes little sense to exclude her from conferences designed to bring some degree of control over nuclear weapons. It is not clear that Peking would accept an invitation to participate in such discussions, but after the explosion of her first nuclear device she suggested a global conference on nuclear control and disarmament, which we promptly rejected. It might be worthwhile for some of the neutral nations to initiate a dialogue aimed at reviving this proposal and drawing the Chinese into a significant role.

3. We should drop our opposition to the admission of China to the United Nations. We need not become an advocate of Peking's admission, but neither should we try any longer to pressure other nations into voting against admission. China may be voted a seat in the United Nations this fall no matter what we do. But this is a matter for the member nations of the UN to decide, free from undue pressures from the United States or other great powers; certainly we should not use our foreign assistance program as an indirect device to buy votes in the General Assembly against the admission of mainland China. Foreign assistance is too costly and serious a business to waste on a lost cause. It is not clear that Peking would accept a seat in the United Nations, but this is not relevant to the basic question of whether or not she should be offered admission.

4. While encouraging self-determination for the people of Formosa, we should indicate our willingness to abide by the judgment of the United Nations as to a possible solution for the Formosan problem. This is the issue that bars serious discussion of China's relationship to both the United Nations

and the United States. Both communist China and Chiang's nationalist regime insist that there is only one China, of which Formosa is a part. The nationalists now hold Formosa as well as the Chinese seat in the United Nations and insist that Peking must not be recognized or admitted to the UN. Peking, on the other hand, insists that Chiang has no legitimate claim to either Formosa or mainland China, and must be expelled from the UN before Peking will enter.

The immediate origin of the Formosa problem was the Cairo Conference of 1943 at which President Roosevelt and Winston Churchill promised Chiang Kai-shek that Formosa would be given to China after the defeat of Japan. The island had been ceded to Japan "in perpetuity" by the Chinese at the end of the Sino–Japanese war in 1895. During the next half century of energetic Japanese rule, Formosa became a developed society with a sense of identity apart from the Chinese mainland. The Formosans eagerly anticipated the end of Japanese rule in the expectation that they would have a more effective political voice in their own affairs as a part of postwar China.

Instead, Chiang's government immediately suppressed all overtures from the Formosans toward representation in the government that emerged after 1945. Formosan political leaders were imprisoned or executed, and the island was invaded by hordes of opportunists from the Chinese mainland, who appropriated all the property that could be carted off or exploited for private gain. Formosan residents, as distinct from those who came from China after World War Two, were excluded from all important political, commercial, and educational positions. When Chiang was defeated by the communists in 1949, he and 2 million supporters fled to Formosa and made the island their fiefdom—ignoring the wishes of the 10 million residents. Heavily supported by U.S. military and economic aid, Formosa has prospered economically, although to this day it knows little democracy. Many of its people, including some who came from China after 1949, now feel the same kind of separate identity from the Chinese mainland that developed during the half century of Japanese rule. There is considerable evidence that Chiang's professed determination to return to the mainland is not shared by many of his subjects. Meanwhile, it seems ironical that the peace of the world is jeopardized by the uncertain status of this little island.

Our only honorable way out of the Formosa dilemma is to foster a situation of self-determination there, combined with a more active United Nations role aimed at an acceptable solution. We cannot lightly turn Formosa over to Peking, since that would be a betrayal of both the Chinese who fled there after 1949 and of the Formosans' hope for a hand in their own governance. Neither can we hope to maintain permanent credibility for the fiction that Chiang will recover control of mainland China from his island base.

Peking can be expected to oppose any arrangement that does not simply turn the island over to her. Chiang will object to any proposed election supervised by outsiders, on the grounds that it would represent meddling in the internal affairs of Formosa. The nationalist regime has never had a popular mandate, although it has developed an election process in local administration under the Formosa Provincial Government. We should applaud this development and put our influence behind any and all procedures that permit the people of Formosa to determine their own government and in time establish their independence by democratic means.

Should not the Formosa Provincial Government begin to play a greater role in administration of the island's economic affairs? Should we not expect the nationalist government and the provincial government eventually to merge in the interests of greater efficiency and responsiveness to popular interests? Aging President Chiang, through his controlled nationalist legislature, has just appropriated increased power, assumed another six-year term, and designated his successors; these are decisions that should ideally be made by the people of Formosa in genuine elections.

If our moral support of the election process is accompanied by a clear reaffirmation of our commitment to defend the island, it could not be charged that we were abandoning our allies and the containment of mainland China. We should make clear that we will not tolerate Chinese aggression, nor would we ever permit Chiang and his Nationalist followers to

be handed over to Peking. Nationalist mainlanders and Formosans alike should enjoy the rights of citizenship equally in
an independent, democratic Formosan state. In such a situation, the world could see that self-determination was a fact
because all the people on Formosa could participate in full
political life.

Since our policy toward Formosa has been widely questioned in the international community, it would be wise for
us to place the entire issue before the United Nations. We
could indicate our willingness to abide by the decisions of the
Assembly with the understanding that the wishes of the
Formosans would be considered and that adequate security
arrangements would be worked out. This would place on the
members of the United Nations the responsibility for finding
an acceptable answer to the Formosan dilemma rather than
creating the impression that America is blocking a solution.
We should make clear that we are willing to live not only with
a "One China" or "Two Chinas" policy, but that we would be
happy to see a "One China–One Formosa" solution with maximum self-determination for the people of Formosa.

Steps Toward Communication

Aside from such diplomatic questions as the recognition of
China, her entrance to the United Nations, and the status of
Formosa, there are a number of other areas in which U.S.
initiatives might encourage a better relationship between ourselves and the Chinese. In April, 1965, the United States
Chamber of Commerce unanimously called upon our government "to more effectively open channels of communication
with the people" of mainland China. U.S. Chamber President
Robert Gerholz, who favors trade, discussion, and cultural exchange with the Chinese, said at that time: "It makes no sense
for the United States not to be in touch with a country of 700
million people." He added: "Any time you can get people
around a conference table . . . I prefer it to bombing and
going to war."

1. In that spirit, we could encourage an exchange with

China of scholars, journalists, businessmen, artists, educators, farmers, scientists and tourists. Both China and the United States could profit from an exchange of scientific and technical information in such fields as weather modification, population control, agricultural development, and medical research. Such a policy would avoid the kind of foolish decision that recently prevented us from accepting a rare Chinese Panda bear that a friendly Australian wished to donate to an American zoo. One wonders if Chinese Pandas would really infect us with a dangerous communist virus!

President Johnson acted wisely in his recent decision to permit American scholars to study in China and to grant visas to Chinese scholars applying for study in the United States. Whether or not Peking will admit our scholars or grant passports to her scholars in the immediate future is questionable, but at least we have taken a first step toward opening the ignorance curtain.

Specifically, I would suggest that two or more of our great universities, perhaps Harvard and the University of California, and two or more institutions of higher learning in neutral countries, assemble a task force of medical or other specialists and offer through the neutralist universities to send them to China on an exchange basis.

The Pugwash group of scholars that have had such striking success in establishing private technical communication with their Soviet counterparts, even during the roughest cold war period, might be asked to apply themselves to reaching Chinese scholars on terms not offensive to Peking.

Institutions such as South Dakota State University or Iowa State University might be asked to host a conference on agricultural problems and techniques to which Chinese experts could be invited along with other participants. These universities are so located that visits to nearby farms would give the Chinese observers an opportunity to communicate directly with our farmers and view the operation of typical American farms.

2. We could emphasize our willingness to increase communications with the Chinese by eliminating the requirement of special passports to China and other nations. Any adult citizen should be allowed to travel at his own discretion when-

ever he can secure a visa. The right to travel should be a basic right of American citizens.

For a time, prior to 1960, Peking seemed to be interested in negotiating an exchange of newsmen with the United States. Since then, the Chinese have said that progress on this and other issues must await settlement of the Formosan problem. Some fifty U.S. journalists have validated passports for China, but only Edgar Snow and a farm expert who was inadvertently issued a visa in Helsinki have been admitted. For the United States to drop the travel ban on all citizens would make our own principles clearer and more confident, while placing the responsibility on Peking for roadblocks to communications and travel.

3. We should open the door for trade in nonstrategic materials and cease our pressures to discourage other nations from trading with the Chinese. Sixty-eight per cent of China's trade is now with our "free world" allies. Japan has replaced Russia as China's major trading partner—an arrangement that benefits both Japan and China and makes China less dependent on the communist world.

Since no responsible Chinese official has proposed increased trade with the United States, there is no immediate likelihood of a flourishing trade with us. But the removal of present blanket prohibitions would enable individual U.S. traders to deal with China much as they have with Russia and eastern Europe. Today, the only goods that cross borders are publications and printed material between libraries and various institutes, but this trickle might flow faster if present U.S. regulations were relaxed so that we might trade with the Chinese on the same basis as we do the Russians. This would not weaken American security, but it could introduce China's agricultural and industrial managers to American goods and methods. It could stimulate demands among their engineers and technicians for greater access to U.S. technical data. It could open the door for sales of wheat and other surplus crops to a nation that undoubtedly contains many hungry mouths.

In recent years China's fast-growing population, unfavorable weather, and the failure of the "great leap forward" have resulted in large grain shortages. As a consequence, Peking has purchased huge quantities of wheat and other cereals from Canada, Australia, and France. Indeed, Canadian farmers and exporters are experiencing an economic boom as a result of sizable sales to China and the Soviet Union. The Canadian, Australian and French governments have relaxed acreage controls, utilized surpluses, and stimulated their agricultural and related industries. The Chinese grain purchases have been a new-found gold mine to our wheat exporting allies. The United States, in contrast, is struggling to control the output of farmers by acreage controls, land retirement schemes, and other expensive devices. We have sought to isolate our accumulated surpluses in government-financed storage programs. While putting up with tight acreage restrictions and price-depressing surpluses, farmers have been blamed for the high public cost of the control program. Meanwhile, the entire economy has suffered from a restricted and depressed agriculture.

Given these factors, would it not be in the nation's interest to lift some of the restrictions that have foreclosed U.S. grain sales in China and other parts of the communist world? Is there really any reason to believe that a well-fed communist is more dangerous than a hungry one?

Such trade would obviously be of economic benefit to us in increased income and a sharply improved balance of payments. If the political blocks to trade could be removed, American farmers could expect to sell a quarter of a billion dollars of grain to the Chinese each year. This would not only enrich our farmers, it would mean new economic stimulus and greater sales of farm machinery, farm supplies, shipping and materials of all kinds. Idle acres and abandoned farms would once again begin to produce and rural communities would feel strengthened purchasing power. The potential impact of a flourishing trade with a nation approaching a billion people is difficult to comprehend. Such trade is also a sound political and moral position for the nation in demonstrating the efficiency of our agriculture and industry and our recognition that even political rivals should not be denied the choice to purchase food and other nonstrategic materials that we have in abundance.

The foregoing are a few of the steps the United States could take with no serious risk that might strengthen our security by encouraging more amicable relations with the people of China. They would not lessen the effective military containment of China, but might in fact make it more practical. We have neither the mission nor the capacity to play God in Asia by a unilateral U.S. police operation. Vietnam should have taught us the futility of this role. But an enlightened U.S. policy that recognized China's reasonable diplomatic, economic, and cultural interests might not only lessen Chinese belligerence; it would also be more inclined to win the approval of Japan, India, Pakistan, the Soviet Union, and our western European allies, whose support will be required for any effective determination of China's legitimate role in Asia.

The suggested steps should make clear that while we would resist any military aggression by the Chinese, we want to see them prosper in a climate of peace. While we do not approve of their system of government for ourselves, we could wish them continued progress in their efforts to organize and develop their vast country and conquer its staggering problems. The Chinese have accomplished much of value in a few short years—improving the status of women, lifting the educational level of the people and eliminating most of the crime, prostitution, and corruption of their great cities. In spite of droughts, floods, heavy population pressures, and organizational mistakes, they have vastly improved their food distribution so that large-scale starvation has been prevented. Scientific, technical and economic advancements have been remarkable. All of these worthwhile accomplishments, achieved without substantial aid from other countries, are worthy of our respect. It is true that they have been accompanied by a high degree of regimentation, but as Professor Lucian W. Pye has observed: "The mere assignment of ruling what may become half the world's population with only a small fraction of the world's resources will compel Chinese leaders to keep their society on a tight leash."

It is not likely that China would respond favorably to U.S. initiatives in the immediate future. Her leaders are not presently in a happy mood. China's heavy-handed interference in Africa, Indonesia, and Cuba has been rebuffed by the people of those states, which she thought were logical allies. She has suffered a bitter estrangement from the Soviet Union. Aside from the deep scars of a century of western humiliation, her leaders are haunted by the memories of "The Long March" and decades of civil strife and misrule. They bitterly resent the U.S. nuclear power that encircles them—to say nothing of the escalating war in Vietnam.

For these and other reasons, China may react in a hostile, if not hysterical manner to U.S. overtures. UN Secretary-General U Thant has said that the Chinese leadership is gripped by the anxieties of a nervous breakdown. If that analysis is correct, it is all the more urgent that we take reasonable steps to quiet their fears. Certainly, we will not make China less belligerent by answering hysteria with hysteria, or name-calling by name-calling. When the Chinese recite our faults and ignore our virtues, it does not make them more reasonable for us to display the same blind emotionalism. If they have a distorted image of us, that does not make it in our interest to live with a distorted vision of them.

We must be prepared for rebuffs, insults, and misinterpretations of our motives. But with enough patience, an imaginative policy aimed at drawing China into the family of nations should bear more fruit than a policy designed to isolate, antagonize, and hamper her development. As the exponents of freedom, we would do well to remember the words of Judge Learned Hand:

> The spirit of liberty is the spirit which is not too sure that it is right; the spirit of liberty is the spirit which seeks to understand the minds of other men and women; the spirit of liberty is the spirit which weighs their interests alongside its own without bias . . .

Senator Fulbright has brilliantly highlighted the danger of following "old myths" rather than "new realities." If, however, one considers current tendencies to substitute military power and diplomatic rigidity for the eternal imperatives of brotherhood and reconciliation, it may be that our dilemma stems from substituting new myths for old realities. But regardless of the angle of vision on our growing quandary in Asia, we need to develop that reasonableness of mind, that "spirit of liberty," which gives force to the words: "We must change to master change."

■ *One of the most fascinating chapters in American po-*
litical history has been the gradually mounting dissent
since 1964 against American military involvement in
Vietnam. From the outset of our support of the French
in their efforts to crush Ho Chi Minh, 1946–1954, there
had been sporadic criticisms of American policy in
southeast Asia. But such dissent was confined largely to
a few sophisticated journals and a handful of scholars.

The Vietnam policy dissent in the Senate really got
underway in early 1964 with a series of bluntly worded
speeches by Oregon Senator Wayne Morse and Alaska
Senator Ernest Gruening. Morse, one of the most power-
ful orators ever to serve in the Senate, delivered his first
major attack on American policy in Vietnam on March
4, 1964. From that day on, he bombarded the Adminis-
tration with blast after blast against the illegality, the
immorality, and the foolishness of the Vietnam inter-
vention.

Gruening, a tough-minded, grizzled old warrior with
a profound abhorrence of what he described as our
"Vietnam folly," delivered his first major indictment
on March 10, 1964. In speech after speech, he struck
hard at the whole range of diplomatic, legal, and polit-
ical assumptions behind Administration policy in
Vietnam.

The Morse–Gruening indictments of our Vietnam
policy were considered overly harsh and strident by
many members of the Senate, although a number of
senators privately agreed with much of what they said.
Their arguments made sense to me, although I feared
that the harshness of their approach would create a
negative Administration reaction and might alienate po-
tential dissenters within the Senate. Morse and Gruen-
ing, however, have earned a high place in history for
their candor, courage and wisdom in speaking out early
and clearly on the Vietnam issue.

These two senators cast the only "no" votes against
the Bay of Tonkin resolution of August 1964—a reso-
lution later interpreted by the Administration as a kind
of blank-check congressional endorsement for the sub-
sequent escalation of the war. Senator Gaylord Nelson,
a thoughtful Vietnam critic, seriously considered at-
taching an amendment to the Tonkin resolution to

limit its application, but was persuaded not to do so by the floor manager of the resolution, Senator William Fulbright, who sincerely believed, as did nearly the entire Senate, that the resolution involved no significant change in American policy. Many senators voted for the resolution as a courtesy to the President at a time when he was being accused by his challenger, presidential candidate Barry Goldwater, of weakness on the Vietnam issue.

In early 1965, Senator Frank Church of Idaho and I opened a new approach to the Vietnam issue by concentrating on a series of carefully worded appeals to the Administration to undertake a negotiated settlement of the war. Instead of indicting the President, we sought to persuade him to offer to begin negotiations to end the war. Our early suggestions were rebuffed by the Secretary of State and others with the assertion that there was nothing to negotiate until Hanoi stopped what it was doing in South Vietnam.

I had made my first Senate criticism of our Vietnam policy on September 24, 1963—several months prior to the Morse–Gruening indictments—but these early remarks were "lost" in a lengthy speech on the general theme of reversing the arms race. My first major Vietnam policy criticism came in a Senate speech on January 15, 1965, followed by joint efforts with Senator Church on February 17 and 18, 1965. These and subsequent efforts by Church and me led President Johnson to invite us to his office at the White House the afternoon of April 7, 1965, to tell us that in a speech at Johns Hopkins University that night he would offer to negotiate with Hanoi.

The President's negotiating offer was accompanied by a series of sharp military attacks, however, and was worded in such a manner as to draw an almost certain rejection from Hanoi and the National Liberation Front. Shortly thereafter, Senator Fulbright joined the Vietnam opposition and, as chairman of the Foreign Relations Committee, was soon to become its focal point in the Senate.

In a Senate speech delivered on July 27, 1965, I made what I believe to be the first public formulation of the "enclave" strategy as applied to Vietnam. This *defensive posture—designed to reduce loss of lives on both sides—seemed the most sensible alternative to withdrawal, but to my disappointment, little attention was given to the proposal. General James Gavin later gave his prestigious support to the enclave strategy in a letter to* Harper's *magazine and subsequently in testimony before the Senate Foreign Relations Committee. Since that time the idea of consolidating our troops around the key cities and coastal areas has received considerable discussion; but our strategy has continued to be one of aggressive "search and destroy" operations in pursuit of military victory. As a result, each succeeding year has seen more Americans killed in Vietnam than all the preceding years combined, without noticable improvement in our position.*

All in all, two dozen or more senators—mostly Northern Democrats—were drawn into the Vietnam dissent at one time or another, although the major debate was carried by eight or ten senators. Senate Majority Leader Mike Mansfield, aided by the senior Republican in the Senate, George Aiken, and Kentucky's Senator John Sherman Cooper, played a highly important role in educating the Senate and the nation on the Vietnam issue. One wonders yet why a perceptive, sobering document known as the Mansfield Report—written by Mansfield, Aiken, and several other senators in the fall of 1965 after a tour of southeast Asia—did not lead to a reversal of our Vietnam escalation.

Of my own Vietnam speeches, the one I believe to have been the most significant was delivered on the Senate floor April 25, 1967, and published simultaneously in The Progressive *magazine. I had scheduled the speech for delivery the day after General Westmoreland, the commander of our forces in Vietnam, was to address the American Society of Newspaper Publishers in New York, and just a few days prior to his address to a joint session of Congress. There was every indication that the general was brought back to the United States by the President to end the dissent and unite the country behind the war effort.*

After reading General Westmoreland's contention in New York that the chief barrier to American military victory in Vietnam was the political dissent at

*home, I made a quick but difficult decision to proceed
with my speech and to add an opening section that
takes direct exception to the Administration–Westmoreland effort to silence dissent.*

Vietnam

For several years, a number of senators have warned
against our escalating troop commitment to Vietnam. These
senators, myself, and others, have predicted that each new
escalation of forces on our part would lead to a further escalation on the other side, thus setting the stage for a larger and
bloodier war on the Asian mainland. One of the difficulties
with this formula in a guerrilla war is that ten additional
soldiers from our side can be offset by one soldier on the other
side, which gives the enemy an enormous advantage in a war
of attrition. This is the very course that most of our best generals have warned against for many years.

The predictions and the warnings of these generals and
the Senate critics have proved to be largely correct. The glittering military solutions of the war hawks, on the other hand,
have proved to be wrong. Now in their frustration, the hawks
are trying to blame the failure of their policy on their critics.

I do not blame General Westmoreland for his speech in
New York, because obviously he is doing, whether in Vietnam
or in New York, exactly what he is told to do by his Commander in Chief.

From General Westmoreland on down, we have in Vietnam our finest soldiers and marines. They are brave men, and
they have fought with valor and distinction, as American

Speech in the United States Senate, April 25, 1967.

fighting men have always fought. This only adds to the heart-ache of those of us who feel that these brave men are in Viet-nam because of the shortsightedness of our political and diplo-matic policymakers. In trying to imply that it is American dissent that is causing the Vietnamese opposition to continue the war, the Administration is only confessing the weakness of its own case by trying to silence its critics and confuse the American people.

It is not the impact of the dissent on Hanoi that worries the Administration; it is the fact that the dissenters have ex-posed the contradictions, the falsehood, and the resulting credibility gap that surrounds Administration policy.

Hanoi knows very well that America is not going to sur-render or withdraw from this war. Hanoi knows very well that not a single U.S. senator has advocated either U.S. surrender or U.S. withdrawal.

What we have advocated is that the Administration quit widening the war; that the Administration quit sending more and more American boys to do the job that ought to be done by Asian boys. Although we have opposed sending American men to Vietnam, we have not urged withdrawal of those men until a satisfactory settlement has been negotiated.

Frustrated by the failure of the escalation policy to produce anything other than a bloodier war, as we warned it would do, the Administration policymakers are now trying to blame their failure on those who have warned them all along that they were playing with fire.

Knowing full well the political hazards involved in ques-tioning the Administration's wartime policy, I can only warn again today that the new level of escalation marked by our bombing of the North Vietnamese airfields has brought us one step closer to a major war involving the legions of China backed by the enormous firepower of Soviet Russia. Thus, I do not intend to remain silent in the face of what I regard as a policy of madness, which sooner or later will envelop Ameri-can youth by the millions in a war without end.

Our deepening involvement in Vietnam represents the most tragic diplomatic and moral failure in our national ex-perience. The mightiest nation in history—a nation with a glorious democratic tradition based on the dignity and brotherhood of man—is, with allegedly good motives, devastating an impoverished little state and ravishing the people whose freedom we would protect. In the process we are sacrificing many of our bravest young men, wasting valuable resources, and threatening the peace of the world. We are being pulled step by step into a jungle quicksand that may claim our sons and the sons of Asia for years to come. This is the path of which the late Douglas MacArthur said:

> Anyone who commits American forces to a land war in Asia ought to have his head examined.

If the war continues on its present course, our dreams of a Great Society and a peaceful world will turn to ashes. Vietnam is degenerating into a defeat for America whether we "win" or "lose" on the battlefield; indeed, the more complete our military conquest, the more tragic our real loss may become.

What will we have really won if we succeed at long last in killing enough Vietnamese to bring us victory on the battlefield?

I have no doubt about the capacity of this greatest and most powerful of all countries to eventually score a military decision of sorts in Vietnam.

Shortly before he was killed with a U.S. marine unit in Vietnam, the learned Bernard Fall, whose expertise on southeast Asia was, in my opinion, unequaled, had an interview in Saigon with a reporter named Bronson P. Clark. I should like to read one paragraph from that interview:

> "The one overwhelming fact about this situation," Fall told me, "which makes all considerations of ideology or politics pale, is the enormous might of American firepower." Operation Cedar Falls in the Iron Triangle twenty miles northwest of Saigon was fresh in his mind: "It looked like giant steel claws had raked the jungle." He spoke of the ground effect of fourteen consecutive B-52 raids which the triangle had received during the operation. "But remember, when it was all over the Vietcong struck again and from the Iron Triangle. That is the real story of this war. The Americans can destroy but they cannot pacify. They

may 'win' the war but it will be the victory of the grave-yard."

Our policy in Vietnam has been rationalized by a crude misreading of history and a distortion of our most treasured ideals. There was no American interest, no issue of political freedom, no moral imperative that called for sending our troops and bombers into Vietnam. Freedom is worth fight-ing for, but it cannot be achieved through an alliance with unpopular forces abroad that deny freedom. Communism is a force hostile to American ideals, but we do not meet its challenge by forcing an American solution on a people still in search of their own national identity. Mao Tse-tung may have claimed that "power grows out of the barrel of a gun," but that has not been the chief source of American power in the world, and it does not answer the basic yearning of the people of Asia. After all the dead are counted—Ameri-can and Vietnamese—and the countryside is laid waste, what will we then have accomplished? Could it be that having sown the wind, we shall reap the whirlwind?

We fight in Vietnam, not for any enduring objective; rather, we fight because of a highly questionable notion that this is the only honorable course. Implicit in our Vietnam involvement is an assumption that we may be ordained to settle the struggles and determine the ideology of the people of Asia.

We fight, also, perhaps, to save the professional reputation of policy planners who have recommended a series of steps, each one seemingly prudent and restrained, yet each one in-exorably setting in motion the next step to a larger war. Our policymakers have inadvertently placed American power in opposition to basic forces, including the currents of revolu-tionary nationalism and social ferment convulsing much of Asia. Our course has run afoul of the desire of many of the Vietnamese people to escape outside interference, whether French, Japanese, Chinese, or American. We seem to be trying to demonstrate that American power can enable unpopular, incompetent regimes in Saigon to offset a widespread insurrec-tion; that bombing bridges, roads, and oil depots—and now the airfields of North Vietnam—will somehow compensate for the weak government in the South.

For years we have been told that some new show of American strength would bring the other side to the negotiating table. Instead, a Vietnamese civil conflict has been transformed gradually into a cruel international war. Our leaders talk about stopping aggression from the north, but this was a struggle among groups of Vietnamese until we intervened.

We seem bent upon saving the Vietnamese from Ho Chi Minh even if we have to kill them and demolish their country to do it. As the native people survey bombed-out villages, women and children burned by napalm, rice crops destroyed, and cities overrun with our military personnel, they are doubtless saying secretly of the Vietcong guerrillas and of the American forces, "A plague on both your houses."

The responsibility for our present predicament in southeast Asia cannot be placed on any one man or on any single Administration or agency of government. Its roots go back more than twenty years, to four Administrations as well as Congress and the American public. Senators must bear a portion of the blame for the drift of our policy in Vietnam, for we have been slow to speak clearly or even to ask hard questions about obvious contradictions, poor intelligence, and false prophecies involving the highest officials of our government. Dissent in Congress and the nation has been sharp and frequent in recent years, but it has come late in the day.

Many of the Senate's most influential members, including the chairmen of powerful committees, have believed for years that the United States made a serious mistake in intervening in Vietnam—first by trying to defeat the Vietnamese independence struggle led by Ho Chi Minh against imperial France, and second, by fostering a divided Vietnam leading to civil conflict after the expulsion of the French. Yet, upon this privately admitted error a strange syllogism has been constructed:

—The United States erred in entering and enlarging the Vietnamese struggle.

—We are, nevertheless, now deeply involved in that struggle.

—Therefore, we have no recourse except to see it through at any cost, or force the other side to negotiate on our terms.

It is a strange piece of logic, indeed, that holds that, once committed to error, we must compound the error by more of the same, to salvage the original mistake. It would seem more reasonable, having accepted the premise of error in our involvement, to avoid further widening of the war while devoting our most imaginative efforts to finding a way to end the killing.

Before we take any further steps toward a larger war—and I notice in the press that our commander is said to be asking for considerably more troops in Vietnam—or before we undertake any new ventures of this kind elsewhere in the world, I would hope that we will reexamine the assumptions that have involved us in what I believe to be a mistaken course. Perhaps the only positive benefit that may come from an otherwise melancholy venture is for us to see the errors of this one clearly enough to avoid being drawn into another one. To assist in stimulating such a reexamination, I make the following indictments of our Vietnam policy:

1. Our Vietnam policymakers have distorted history to justify our intervention in a civil conflict supposedly to defend a free nation against external aggression from another nation; actually we are backing a dictatorial group in Saigon against a competing group backed by a dictatorial regime from the north.

2. Our Vietnam policymakers are unwittingly advancing the cause of communism while seeking to contain it.

3. While orally calling for negotiations, we are practicing military escalation and diplomatic rigidity in such fashion as to foreclose negotiations.

4. Our policymakers have frequently misled the American public, the result being a serious loss of credibility for the U.S. government.

5. We are wasting human and material resources needed for the revitalization of our society.

6. We are jeopardizing essential U.S. foreign policy interests, including a promising improvement in east–west relations.

7. We bypassed the United Nations until the eleventh hour and have disregarded the opinion and the sensibilities of the international community.

8. We are weakening America's moral position and beclouding American idealism.

9. We are creating at home a climate of intimidation designed to silence dissent and meaningful discussion of policy.

This is a grave indictment. I will summarize briefly the facts and arguments that substantiate these charges.

1. The historical rationalization of our Vietnam intervention is based on the Munich analogy or "the domino theory." At Munich, in 1938, the western allies failed to stand up to Hitler's demand for a piece of Czechoslovakia. The result of this surrender was a series of aggressions leading to World War Two. In Vietnam—so the theory goes—we are faced with another Hitler in the form of Ho Chi Minh, or perhaps Moscow or Peking working through Ho Chi Minh. If only Ho or his backers can be stopped in Vietnam, we will have averted another Munich and saved mankind from world war three. As one of our soldiers was reported to have said, according to a newspaper in my state:

> We are fighting in Vietnam so we won't have to have foxholes and barbed wire entanglements on the Main Street of Aberdeen, South Dakota.

It is said that if we do not crush Ho, his control of Vietnam will topple such other dominoes as Laos, Thailand, Cambodia, Burma, the Philippines, and perhaps India, Pakistan, Australia, and Japan, and then on to Hawaii and San Francisco. We are left to wonder how a flotila of Vietnamese or Chinese junks is going to get by the Seventh Fleet en route to San Francisco.

This, I think, is a piece of historical nonsense. There is no analogy between Munich and Vietnam, and countries are not dominoes.

Hitler was a madman commanding the world's mightiest military machine—a machine with the mobility, the offensive power, and the assigned mission of leaping across national frontiers until the world was conquered. At Munich, he directly threatened Czechoslovakia, a highly developed democratic state that was ready to fight for its survival with any indication of western support.

Ho Chi Minh, doubtless guilty of many sins, has nevertheless devoted most of his public life to winning independence for his country. A confirmed Marxist, he is more significantly an ardent nationalist, bound less by the claims of international communism than by Vietnamese nationalism. He is far less interested in what Peking or Moscow want than he is in what he wants for his own country.

During World War Two, Ho stood with the United States against the Japanese and assisted American flyers shot down over Japanese-held jungle areas. With the end of World War Two he resisted French efforts to regain colonial control of his people. After eight years of fighting, he defeated the French and emerged a national hero. At the Geneva Conference of 1954, he agreed to end the fighting, withdraw his forces north of a temporary cease-fire line at the 17th parallel, and await an election two years hence that doubtless would have led to his election as leader of a united Vietnam. Former President Eisenhower has written that in 1954 after expelling the French, Ho had the support of at least 80 per cent of the Vietnamese people, both North and South.

But the promised elections were blocked by Premier Ngo Dinh Diem, whom we were instrumental in installing in South Vietnam. Of equal significance—and this is sometimes lost sight of—Diem cut off all trade and other relationships with North Vietnam, and ruthlessly suppressed his internal opposition.

I remember that the late Bernard Fall, whom I referred to a while ago, said that the cutting off of trade between the North and South had as much to do in causing the conflict that eventually developed as anything else.

This was the background for the Vietcong revolt in the South, aided by Ho Chi Minh from the North. Although marked by bloodshed and violence, it is scarcely analogous to Hitler's attempted global conquest in moving against international frontiers with a mighty military machine. The insurrection in Vietnam grew out of local conditions, which pitted one group of Vietnamese against another. Even if there had never been such a country as China, the probability is that that revolt would have taken place.

Ho Chi Minh heads one of the smallest and most impoverished states in the world. Neither in capacity nor by inclination can he be seriously seen as a Hitler-type conqueror threatening the security of America and the world.

As for the falling dominoes that are said to be marked for "wars of liberation" elsewhere in Asia, and therefore seem to be the rationalization for the enormous commitment we are making there—it is clear that the challenge to them is not a Hitler or a Ho from the outside, but their own domestic political, economic, and social problems. A country that builds a government responsive to the needs of the citizenry—that faces up to the internal problems of misrule, injustice, and human misery need have little fear of falling victim to a "war of liberation." A government that ignores these fundamental concerns of its people as the dictators of South Vietnam have done is headed for trouble and does not deserve to be saved—indeed, it probably cannot be saved—by American soldiers.

The late Winston Churchill, who predicted the subsequent aggression of Hitler if he were not stopped at Munich, just as clearly warned in 1954 against any intervention in Vietnam by Britain or the United States. He saw no analogy between Ho and Hitler, and flatly rejected the appeal of Secretary of State Dulles in the spring of 1954 that Britain and the United States should intervene against Ho on the side of the French. It is regrettable that the world did not listen to Churchill before Munich; it is also regrettable that we did not follow his warning against the Vietnam intervention.

One final note of irony in the Munich fallacy is the testimony by our ally in Saigon, General Ky, that his only political hero is Adolf Hitler.

2. To contain Communist Chinese influence and power in Asia, we have set up a series of unpopular dictators in Saigon. Ignoring Vietnam's deep-seated historic opposition to China,

we have assumed that since Ho Chi Minh is a communist, he must therefore be a tool of Peking or Moscow.

It is an uncontested historical fact that for a thousand years the people of southeast Asia have resisted the Chinese more than any other outside power.

Actually, the most powerful force moving in Vietnam, as elsewhere in Asia, is nationalism—not international communism. Ho Chi Minh left to his own devices might have united the Vietnamese as an effective buffer against Chinese penetration of southeast Asia. U.S. policy, far from containing Peking or Moscow, is most likely to draw outside communist power and influence into southeast Asia. It may even reunite the feuding communist world.

Since I wrote that statement, there have been all kinds of evidence compiled by our best observers, that that is exactly what is happening. The war is reuniting Peking and Moscow in a common policy with reference to southeast Asia.

The destruction of South Vietnamese villages by American bombers and the growing occupation of city and countryside by American forces, raises the unpopular specter of a western occupation again and plays into the hands of communist propagandists all over Asia. In the North, American bombers are pounding away at the North Vietnamese economic and industrial strength. The resulting chaos—or vacuum—is hardly calculated to provide a formidable barrier to Chinese penetration.

3. Our diplomacy before, during and after the Geneva Conference of 1954 has been narrow and self-defeating. For years we made no effort to negotiate or even offer to negotiate an end to the violence. When Ho Chi Minh indicated in 1964 to the Secretary General of the United Nations, U Thant, that he was ready to talk about a settlement, we rejected this opportunity as we have rebuffed other peace feelers before and since.

The Johnson Administration has insisted it is prepared to embark on "unconditional discussions." Thus, on April 27, 1967, President Johnson said:

> I will talk to any government, anywhere, any time *without any conditions,* and if they doubt our sincerity, let them test us.

When tested, however, as it has been on a number of occasions, the Administration has insisted on conditions—and pretty harsh ones at that. Some of the conditions would, in effect, virtually require the prior capitulation of the other side. This was the central fact that emerged from President Johnson's celebrated letter to Ho Chi Minh in February, a letter that far from representing a new and more moderate approach to peacemaking was, in fact, a hardening of our previous position in terms of the conditions we demanded of Hanoi.

4. The American people have been given in the past decade a bewildering array of false assurances, contradictory interpretations, and mistaken predictions about Vietnam. We were assured that our role would be limited to an advisory function—that this was a war that the Vietnamese people must win or lose. Time after time, top Administration officials contended that this was basically a political struggle that could be decided in Saigon's favor only if the government there could draw together enough grassroots support to offset the guerrillas. We were repeatedly assured that American troops and bombers could not solve that problem and in fact would make it worse. For example, speaking on June 12, 1966, just a few days before the first bombing of Hanoi and Haiphong, the U.S. Army Chief of Staff, Gen. Harold K. Johnson, said:

> It would be foolish to expand the war and destroy North Vietnam's economic and military capabilities since this would only double the price of the war because the United States would have to ultimately rebuild what it destroyed.

Yet, only days later, we began doing exactly what General Johnson had said it would be foolish to do. Repeatedly, administration spokesmen have explained in vigorous terms the limits of our policy and our operations in Vietnam only to have those limits abruptly exceeded before the words had died away. Defense Secretary Robert S. McNamara's and Secretary of State Dean Rusk's major pronouncements on the war have been marked by one consistent quality—they have all proved to be wrong.

In the 1964 presidential campaign, millions of Americans rejected Senator Goldwater's prescription for victory in Vietnam through bombing, jungle defoliation, and a major escalation of American forces. President Johnson and his top Cabinet officers built a convincing case against bombing and the escalation of American ground forces. "We seek no wider war" was the winning slogan of 1964.

Yet, the mandate for peace of 1964 has been translated into the Goldwater prescription on the installment plan. Little wonder that the Administration is faced with a credibility gap as wide as the Grand Canyon.

If one were to attempt a balance sheet on the costs and benefits of our Vietnam venture, high on the cost side would be the planting of doubt and resentment leading to a loss of faith in government on the part of many of our people, especially the youth. One of the invaluable sources of national strength is the capacity to enlist the enthusiastic support of the young for essential national interests. To blunt that enthusiasm and vital faith in the reliability and fundamental honesty of our government is a grievous blow to a democratic society.

5. There are other incalculable costs to America and to the world that stem from Vietnam. We are now pumping federal funds into the war effort at a rate of over $2 billion monthly. This is a serious drain on our balance of payments, our dollar, and our fiscal health. It represents money urgently needed to rebuild our decaying, explosive, riot-ridden city slums; to strengthen educational, recreational, and employment opportunities in rural America; to clean up our polluted rivers and streams. It would be ironic, indeed, if we devoted so heavy a proportion of our resources to the pacification of Vietnam that we were unable to pacify Los Angeles, Chicago, and Harlem.

6. It may be that the greatest cost of our Vietnam involvement is its regrettable impact on other vital foreign policy interests of the United States. The improved relations with the Soviet Union that followed the sobering Cuban missile crisis of 1962 gave promise of a détente between the world's two great nuclear powers. Likewise, the fragmentation of the

international communist bloc opened the way for new U.S. initiatives. The reaction against heavy-handed Chinese interference in Africa, Indonesia, and elsewhere suggested further opportunities for a sensitive, flexible U.S. policy. In eastern Europe, the so-called Soviet satellites have seemed to beckon for better relations with the west. Progress toward nuclear control was promised by the limited test ban treaty of 1963.

All of these hopeful and challenging foreign policy opportunities have been threatened on thwarted by the fast-deepening U.S. preoccupation with the war in Vietnam. Our policy planners, the Congress, and the American people are devoting so much energy and attention to one tiny corner of southeast Asia that we tend to lose sight of the fast-changing global panorama that is moving before our eyes.

7. The United States was founded by men who declared our national independence with "a decent respect for the opinions of mankind." Our nation, 170 years later, took the lead in establishing the United Nations to preserve the peace. On several occasions we worked through United Nations channels to meet international crises—the Arab–Israeli conflict, the Suez crisis, Korea, the Congo, Cyprus, Kashmir, and Yemen. But in Vietnam, we have plunged in alone with only a belated reference to the United Nations.

The United Nations Charter commits us to seek the settlement of disputes through the international machinery of that organization. Our SEATO treaty commits us only to confer with the other treaty signatories on possible action. Yet, in the name of a vague international commitment we fight on in Vietnam with no backing from the United Nations, no broad SEATO support, and, indeed, little support from any source other than a few small states heavily dependent upon our favor. The only important power publicly backing our Vietnam course is Britain, which is dependent upon American support for maintenance of the pound. Even in this instance, Prime Minister Harold Wilson has disassociated his government from our bombing of Haiphong and Hanoi.

8. America's greatest asset in the world has been our democratic tradition, our concept of human dignity, and a humane

society devoted to peace. But Vietnam presents a different view of America. Here the world sees America intervening with massive military power—napalm, artillery, and bombing —on a scale heretofore used only against Nazi Germany and Tojo's Japan in the 1940s. American actions in Vietnam, however well intentioned, do not square with the image of America that the world has traditionally admired.

In November of 1965, I visited a civilian casualty hospital in Danang near the site of one of our largest airbases in Vietnam. The poorly equipped wards were jammed with terribly burned, broken and torn men, women and children, innocent victims of our bombs, napalm and artillery. They lay silently —two persons on each cot—their pained eyes following me as I walked from bed to bed. I wondered that day, as I do now, if this great nation of ours has the right to make so costly a decision on behalf of another people who have already suffered so grievously.

9. Our course in Vietnam does not square with the conscience or the judgment of many thoughtful Americans. But as the tempo of the battle increases and the martial spirit rises, the dissenter will need to draw deeply on his courage. Our official spokesmen have demonstrated a growing resentment toward the doubter and the dissenter. The impression is being created that while freedom of conscience and expression are desirable theoretical principles, they are too dangerous to practice in wartime. Even when the claims of top-level officials prove to be groundless or contradictory, the pressure is on to accept the next pronouncement without question. To challenge the soundness of our policy judgments is more and more being equated with "letting down the boys in Vietnam" or giving aid to Hanoi. It is almost as though we are fighting so intently to secure freedom in Vietnam that we are willing to sacrifice it in America. It is still a regrettable truism that truth is the first casualty in wartime; yet it is in times of national crisis and conflict that America most urgently needs men who will speak out with maximum candor.

For my own part, I reject the assumptions that lie behind our involvement, and I regret each new step toward a deeper involvement. Before we take those fateful additional steps that may lead to Armageddon, I recommend now as I have in the past, but with a new urgency and a deeper concern, that we:

Stop the bombing, North and South; end search-and-destroy offensive sweeps; and confine our military action to holding operations on the ground. Bombing the North has failed to halt or seriously check the flow of troops to the South and may, in fact, have prompted a much greater war effort by Hanoi. Secretary McNamara himself told a Senate committee:

> I don't believe that the bombing . . . has significantly reduced (nor would reduce) the actual flow of men and materiel to the South.

In the South, our bombs have killed or maimed countless numbers of innocent people and alienated others whose support we covet. A defensive holding action in the South, as advocated by Generals Gavin and Ridgway, could be pursued while determined efforts are being made to negotiate a cease-fire. It is the bombing of North Vietnam that presents the greatest obstacle to a settlement and greatest danger of involving Russia or China in the war.

We should clearly state our willingness to negotiate directly with the Vietcong with some recognition that they will play a significant role in any provisional government resulting from a cease-fire and a negotiated settlement.

We should use what influence we have to encourage a more broadly based civilian government in Saigon—a government willing to start discussions with the other side, looking toward arrangements to end the war.

We should advocate an international presence to police a cease-fire, supervise elections, provide an umbrella for the resettlement of Vietnamese concerned about their safety, and arrange for the withdrawal of all outside forces and the conversion of military bases to peacetime uses.

The path to sanity and peace in southeast Asia will not be easy. The way to a larger war is enticing and simple. But before we make that choice, let us recall the words of Virgil:

Easy is the descent to Hell; night and day the gates stand open; but to reclimb the slope and escape to the outer air, this indeed is a task.

But if we can accomplish that task, we should use the Vietnam experience as a guide to future policy. The enormous destruction of life and property in Vietnam, both American and Vietnamese, will have served no useful purpose unless we learn well the lessons that this tragic conflict can teach us. Those lessons, I believe, include the following:

First, conflicts of this kind have historical dimensions that are essentially political, economic, and psychological; they do not respond readily to military force from the outside. Surely, the military might of the United States can subdue little Vietnam, South and North.

But is this what the struggle is all about? I think not. We are confronted in Vietnam with an indigenous guerrilla force that has enjoyed the sympathy or the complicity of much of the local peasantry. The ineffective and unpopular regimes of Saigon have not earned the confidence of their subjects. Urgent priorities, of which land reform is probably the most important, have been ignored. Thus, the destruction of the military power of the guerrillas and of North Vietnam leaves fundamental political and economic problems still festering to set the stage for future conflict or continued tyranny and injustice.

Second, in the future the United States should avoid committing its power to internal struggles of this kind. The factors involved are so complex and confusing that it is beyond the capacity of an outside nation to know which group deserves support and which opposition. In spite of the Administration's strenuous efforts to picture the situation as a war of aggression from the North, it is essentially a civil conflict among various groups of Vietnamese. The Vietcong control is strongest in the delta country of the south, a thousand miles from North Vietnam; and that control is exercised by indigenous forces who enjoy the cooperation of the local peasantry.

Such internal disputes should be fought out by the competing groups without outside interference, or be referred to the United Nations. We have no obligation to play policeman for the world—and especially in Asia, which is so sensitive to heavy-handed interference by even well-meaning white men.

Third, unpopular, corrupt regimes of the kind we have been allied with in Saigon do not deserve to be saved by the blood of American boys. Local governments that have done a good job usually have the confidence of the local citizens. They ordinarily do not have a guerrilla problem and when they do, their own people are loyal enough to the government to take care of the guerrillas instead of depending on us to do that for them.

Even if one assumes that we are faced with a battle for power between Ho Chi Minh of the North and Marshal Ky of the South, there is no clear issue here of tyranny *versus* freedom. Ho is a communist tyrant, but does Marshal Ky with his admiration for Adolf Hitler, represent the kind of ideals and morality that American men should die for?

I have never regretted my service as a bomber pilot in World War Two when we stopped the madmen Hitler, Mussolini, and Tojo. But I do not believe that Vietnam is that kind of testing ground of freedom and free-world security. It is a confusing civil conflict, with no real certainty as to the issues at stake. I do not want my son or other boys to die in that kind of doubtful struggle.

Fourth, those who believe that American military power has an important role to play in the Pacific should return to the once-accepted doctrine of our best generals that we should avoid committing American soldiers to the jungles of Asia. Our power in the Pacific is in naval and air strength as a deterrent against aggression. Local governments must deal with their own guerrilla problems.

Fifth, Congress must never again surrender its power under our constitutional system by permitting an ill-advised, undeclared war of this kind. Our involvement in South Vietnam came about through a series of moves by the Executive branch —each one seemingly restrained and yet each one setting the stage for a deeper commitment. The complex of Administration moves involving the State Department, the CIA, the Pentagon, AID, and various private interests—all of these have played a greater role than has Congress. Congress cannot be very proud of its function in the dreary history of this steadily widening war. That function has been very largely one of acquiescence in little-understood Administration efforts. The surveillance, the debate, and the dissent since 1965, while courageous and admirable, came too late in the day to head off the unwise course charted by our policymakers.

For the future, members of Congress and the Administration will do well to heed the admonition of Edmund Burke, a distinguished legislator of an earlier day:

A conscientious man would be cautious how he dealt in blood.

The Continuing Revolution in America and the World

The Negro Revolution

The Continuing American Revolution

The status of the Negro in America is the most serious moral crisis facing our nation.

I do not believe that any of us can really think that the Negroes' condition is other than the "shame" President Kennedy has called it. We have known for a long time the facts he presented to the nation so movingly last Tuesday night, but we have comforted ourselves with the knowledge that some steps have been taken on behalf of the Negro. To be sure, a series of decisions in the Supreme Court have cleared important ground. Furthermore, the Kennedy Administration has worked harder and accomplished more through executive action for the Negro than any previous Administration.

So, some of us have been amazed to find that in spite of progress, we have misjudged the cry of the Negro for full citizenship. We must swiftly muster all the wisdom and courage we can, for we are going to have to act quickly on a much broader scale. The Negro people have set in motion a moral revolution based on the Judaeo-Christian ethic and the politics of Jefferson and Lincoln. That is the power of the Democratic ideal; which in the long run cannot be denied. It can be resisted, and clubbed, and shot at from ambush, but it cannot be contained, and each new advance will feed new demands until every American is fully free.

"The Continuing American Revolution" is from a speech before the New York State Young Democratic Convention in New York City, June 15, 1963. "The Point of No Return," below, is from a speech in the United States Senate, June 4, 1964.

As Walter Lippmann has put it: "There is, so to speak, a point of no return in a movement for the redress of grievances. That point is where gradual reform and token appeasement become suddenly not only insufficient but irritating. . . . Then, instead of putting up with a little done slowly, there is a demand that much must be done suddenly."

This is one of the enduring lessons of the American Revolution. That revolution was not born of the cruelest oppression in British imperial history. Indeed, the colonies enjoyed a comparatively high degree of freedom and independence. Yet, in a condition far better than others had endured, there suddenly came from the ferment of freedom a demand for independence—a willingness to stake lives, fortunes, and sacred honor on the gamble for liberty. Why?

Certainly, the idea was not born in 1776. It had long been affirmed in the ancient scriptures that the colonial fathers knew so well. Likewise, for centuries prior to 1776, the political and legal expression of the brotherhood of man and the sanctity of the individual had been growing in Anglo–Saxon law. When Jefferson penned the Declaration of Independence, he borrowed heavily from the earlier words of the Englishman John Locke.

The day before our forefathers were Americans, they were Englishmen steeped in English traditions of law and government. Yet, they severed the ties with the mother country. They insisted on the full measure of their heritage. They insisted on being better Englishmen and truer practitioners of English philosophy than King George III desired. Their demands and demonstrations (of which the Boston Tea Party is only the most celebrated) reached a point of no return, the revolution was on, and Englishmen along the eastern shore of this continent became Americans.

I think if we can understand the spirit of 1776, we can better appreciate the rising expectations that are convulsing the American Negro community and the developing continents of the globe.

The American Revolution and countless other historic demands for a redress of grievances all indicate that the cause of freedom is fired by its own gains. The Negro's march toward full acceptance will accelerate rather than diminish with the victories of each passing day. Martin Luther King and James Meredith and Medgar Evers have without question moved the Negro's demand for full citizenship to the point of no return.

What, then, is the next order of business—if we reject the possibility of widespread military or police suppression? I believe it is the legislation that the President is about to propose to the Congress:

1. extension of the Civil Rights Commisison;
2. strengthening of Negro voting rights;
3. empowering the Attorney General to file school desegregation suits; and
4. prohibition of racial discrimination in public places, restaurants, stores, hotels, and theaters.

I earnestly hope that the President will also decide to call for the establishment of a Fair Employment Practices Code.

It will not be easy, but we are going to pass legislation to eliminate the last barriers to equal civil rights for the Negro. There will be a filibuster, and it will be long and bitter. But we're going to win even if we have to stay in session until Christmas. Indeed, we have no right to celebrate the Spirit of Christmas unless by the end of this centennial of the Emancipation, a full charter of civil rights is incorporated in the law of the land.

We are going to succeed because the American people will not tolerate the only remaining alternative, which is a massive suppression on a mounting scale of the Negro and his white friends.

The Negro's demand for civil justice is greatly complicated by his hunger for better jobs and better schools and better housing at a time when all of these are in short supply for both whites and Negroes. The only answer here is a stepped-up U.S. economy leading to full employment, a stronger program of federal assistance to schools, and expansion of home construction.

I am one senator who believes that these domestic needs are so urgent and so fundamental to the strength of our nation that we ought to shift some of our massive military budget to constructive purposes here at home. We now have enough overkill to destroy the Soviet Union many times over. Why not settle for a military capacity along more reasonable lines, and divert a few billion to the desperately needed priorities of jobs, education, health, and housing, for those Negroes and whites who languish at the bottom of our affluent society? There can be no denying the fact that racial tensions are aggravated when there are not enough jobs and houses and schools to meet the nation's needs. Thus, the cry of the Negro for a bigger piece of the national pie has set in motion new pressures for fuller employment in an expanding economy. We should not forget that once the colonists launched the war for independence from England, they unleashed forces that led also to a social revolution of American life.

Even this is not the whole issue in the Negro's challenge, however, and perhaps not the most fundamental. The President has referred to a "moral problem" rooted in our hearts, where laws cannot reach. This is the longing of every human being to be accepted as a person of worth, not because it is the law, but because it is right. I think that in their own way, the Negro demonstrator and his spokesmen are trying to reach this deeper dimension of the racial problem.

We may be better able to comprehend the message of Birmingham and Jackson in 1963 if we see it as a continuance of the forces unleashed at Philadelphia and Botson in 1776. For it seems to me that the Negro is saying to the white man: "If we are not accepted as your brothers, you cannot hold the birthright of America. If we are not free and equal, you cannot be free and equal. If we are not full members of society, your pursuit of happiness is endangered. If America cannot exemplify human dignity and equality at home, how can she hold steady the torch of freedom around the world?"

The Negro, in short, is echoing the words that Adams and Paine and Jefferson dispatched to King George and to their fellow colonists nearly two centuries ago.

I do not press the analogy to suggest that the American Negro wants to withdraw from the Union. The Black Muslim may talk this way, but in so doing, he stands outside the mainstream of Negro life—both religiously and politically; thus, his leadership of his own people is limited to a small fragment. The American Negro longs to be an American first and a Negro second. He has been molded by America's traditions and culture. He has been schooled in the doctrine of freedom and has died for it on foreign battlefields.

The nonviolent resistance of Martin Luther King—the lunch counter sit-ins, the bus rides, the street parades—have been associated with Gandhi. But Gandhi borrowed the idea from Henry David Thoreau and the New Testament. The Negro's capacity to refrain from violence even when he is being kicked in the face stems from the religious and cultural traditions of his American past. It came first from the slave balconies of the churches, then from the segregated "colored church" and from preachers barely literate enough to read the Scriptures and sing the gospel hymns. They were sensitive to the longings of the soul, however, and beyond some Doctors of Divinity they were attuned to that "man of sorrows, acquainted with grief." Out of the depths of his spirit the Negro created indigenous American art—the "spiritual," the "blues," and "jazz."

In this spirit the Negro writer is saying that the frustration that drives the Negro into the streets, the lunch rooms, and the bus terminals is a desperate act of caring about the American ideal. He has been carrying on an unrequited love affair with America until his heart has burst its bounds.

Many voices may be heard in the Negro writer, but I would illustrate with James Baldwin, who has been poignant on the theme of the estrangement of both Negro and white in America from each other and from their past. Baldwin was rebel enough—and like many a white American who became an expatriate to Europe after World War One, he sought out Paris after World War Two.

He found out what the best of his predecessors did—that he had to come home. It is more remarkable in him, though, for he did not know he had a home. From the vantage point of Europe, he found his country. He found out how profoundly American he was. He develops the theme in many places in his *Notes of a Native Son*.

One brilliant essay develops his confrontation with a native African with whom he had tried to identify in order to recover his racial past. He finds it cannot be done. He is alienated from the African; he is an American. A hybrid American perhaps, physically and in every other aspect of life that is dominated by the memory of the auction block, but still American and linked to his white brother:

> Dimly and for the first time there begins to fall into perspective the nature of the roles they have played in the lives and history of each other. Now he is bone of their bone, flesh of their flesh; they have loved and hated and obsessed and feared each other and his blood is in their soil. Therefore he cannot deny them, nor can they ever be divorced.

Baldwin goes on to say that he just cannot explain this to the African. Of course, he must establish himself in relation to a past, but he knows that it must be an American one:

> What time will bring Americans is at last their own identity. It is on this dangerous voyage and in the same boat that the American Negro will make peace with himself and with the voiceless many thousands gone before him.

In a recent television spotlight on the Negro in Washington, a black minister said of his people: "They are too sophisticated to pray, and too angry to laugh." I thought in response that the white man is also "too sophisticated to pray, and too anxious to laugh." The way back will not be easy for either of us, either to the petition for grace on both sides, or the facing of his guilts by the white and the disciplining of his anger by the Negro. It will take us a while to meet and talk and pray as equals. We do not necessarily need to agree upon all matters. Dignity and reason and hopefully a little humor will show the way.

I believe that as both of us renew our heritage, as we relearn our history and tradition, we shall together re-earn freedom. The great Goethe once wrote:

> What you have inherited from your fathers,
> Earn it, in order truly to possess it.

The Reverend S. D. Whitney, Negro minister of Jackson, Mississippi, speaking at a memorial service for the slain Medgar Evers, said: "Somewhere in the dark a sniper waited to play his part as the coward. But bullets do not destroy ideas. Nothing destroys an idea but a better idea. And the best idea is freedom. That is what he was fighting for."

And that is what we are called to do. If we heed that call, old words will be born anew and we will indeed become "One nation, under God, indivisible, with liberty and justice for all."

The Point of No Return

The proof of our unfinished business is in the black ghettos of our great cities of the North, where millions of human beings are living on the edge of despair. They live in stinking, ugly, overcrowded tenements. Their children grow up on the sidewalks and in the alleys, where the law of the jungle prevails. Their schools, churches, businesses, and recreational facilities deteriorate while the whites head for suburbs.

The proof of our unfinished business is also in the South, where the cold-blooded killer of Medgar Evers runs free; where the brutal murderers of four little Alabama Sunday School girls still are on the loose spreading their message of hate and death; where ministers of the gospel are beaten and clubbed because they have had the courage to stand up for the rights of Negro Americans.

The proof of our unfinished business is in Indiana and Wisconsin and Maryland, where a crusading demagogue whose career rests on discrimination against his fellow man was able to secure a sizeable vote in his incredible bid for the Presidency.

We cannot justify our unfinished business with the excuse that we have not yet had time to act.

Last year marked the 100th anniversary of the Emancipation Proclamation, whose unfulfilled hope continues to be our most conspicuous failure in the cause of human dignity, both at home and abroad.

It is no longer possible to separate our domestic condition from our international posture. Thus, no weapon in the communist propaganda arsenal is so damaging as the stark truth about race relations in the United States. In a world of oppressed colored people struggling for new dignity, no amount of millions spent on the Voice of America can offset the louder voice of racial discrimination across our country.

Four out of every five human beings of the globe are non-whites. Since World War Two, they have been largely caught up in an irrepressible demand for national independence. They have sounded the death knell to colonialism and they are now demanding the right to be treated as equals. Their leaders are proud and sensitive and impatient. And they will mock the pretensions of those who preach democracy but practice discrimination.

Passage of the civil rights legislation now before the Senate is the next order of business. The alternative is a rising tide of racial unrest and disturbance.

I think it is quite possible that if the Senate rejects this long-awaited charter of rights, the people of the United States will be plunged into racial strife that will tear apart the fabric of our society. We would then see infuriated minority leaders and inflamed mobs and sulking killers on an unprecedented scale.

Make no mistake about it: there are Negroes who are hoping that this bill will be defeated, thus discrediting the moderates and opening the way for a radicalization of the Negro leadership. Malcolm X recently said: "I intend to prove that you can't get civil rights in this country. . . . The black man is maturing, he is waking up. That is why I say that we will have real violence." I know that there are some senators, too, who want this bill defeated, but they are not hoping for its defeat as ardently as certain Negro radicals who are waiting for a chance to prove that the moderates are wrong.

The Negro moderates who have counseled patience and legal redress would be swept aside by the radicals who preach hate and violence. We would then see the non-violence of Martin Luther King and Roy Wilkins replaced by the direct action of the black racists. Riots, night bombings, assassinations will be the harvest of justice and equality too long postponed.

EPILOGUE

In the years that have passed since I made the two speeches above, we have begun to realize that the road to racial equality will be longer and rockier than we had expected.

In 1964 Congress passed a tough Civil Rights Act, followed in 1965 by the Voting Rights Act. Recently, many of the brightest and most articulate young blacks have derided civil rights legislation as useless. I do not agree. In my judgment, the time and effort we put into breaking the Southern filibuster were well spent, and this legislation, along with related court decisions and executive orders, constitutes significant progress toward racial equality. But to say that progress has been significant is not to say that it has been adequate. It has not. We have broken through many of the legal barriers to equality, but we are now faced with more formidable educational, social, psychological, and economic barriers.

What is usually referred to as "the race problem" is in fact three problems: the white problem, the black problem, and the poverty problem.

The white problem is white racism. Although it is more severe in the deep South than elsewhere, racism is a prominent feature of the society and politics of every city and every state in the Union. I know of no city without a section or a suburb closed to blacks. We have no black governors and only one black senator, and we have never had a black President or Vice-President. The building-trades union that does not practice discrimination is the exception rather than the rule. High executive positions in most of our major corporations are rigidly closed to blacks, as are the recreational and social organizations to which these executives belong. Far too many black Americans have been subjected to insulting and totally unwarranted discriminatory behavior on the part of the police.

The polls show that most white Americans feel blacks are

pressing for too much progress too quickly. These whites are saying, in effect, "In order to avoid disturbing our sensibilities, we want you to have an inferior education, work at a job far below your ability, confine yourself to the worst neighborhoods in the country, and in general lead a subhuman existence. And we want your children to live the same way. But don't take it too hard; things will be better for your grandchildren . . . or maybe your great-grandchildren. You must give us time to get used to it."

This attitude is indefensible.

For hundreds of years, black Americans have been told implicitly and explicitly that they are inferior to whites, and they have accepted it. Culturally, America is a white nation. Not only are most of our citizens descended from Europeans; our institutions, customs, and laws are based on the European. With the exception of their music, black Americans have been able to retain little of their original African culture. From Crispus Attucks to Martin Luther King, Jr. and Malcolm X, those blacks who have made their mark on American history have done so in the European manner, not the African. They have worn European-American clothes, eaten European-American food, used European-American technology, and communicated in the English language.

Blacks have taken on the life-style of the white, but their color prevents them from forgetting that they did not develop this life-style, that it was forced upon them. This is inevitable, but it is traumatic. A black child goes to church and studies a Bible in which God, Jesus, the angels, and almost all of the characters are white. He goes to school and studies the history of white people. Advertisements, filmed and televised fiction, the newspapers—all of these say to him over and over that America is a white nation, and he knows he is not white.

It is not surprising, then, to find our blacks believing deep down in their own inferiority, to find blacks attempting to literally or figuratively deny their background, and to find light-skinned blacks looking down on darker blacks. Neither is it surprising to find many young blacks vigorously rejecting all of this.

Many white liberals have been bewildered by the new insistence on the term "black" instead of "Negro." After all, doesn't "Negro" mean "black"? But to an Afro-American, "Negro" reminds him of a century of second-class citizenship. Moreover, he sees "Negro" as a euphemism, as a polite attempt on the part of whites to avoid the cruder term "black" and thus to avoid offending him. But this implies there is something offensive in a reference to a black person's color. The proud young blacks do not see it that way. They accept themselves as they are, and they rightly resent any imputation, however unintentional, of black inferiority. They are overcoming the psychological battering that white racism has inflicted upon their parents.

In this process of overcoming, some of them have yielded to the temptation to strike back violently at the society that has oppressed them. A few have fallen into a black racism comparable to the crudest white racism in its blind senselessness and its debilitating effect upon its practitioner. Some have rioted, burned, and looted, thereby destroying their own homes and those of their brothers, and stimulating a white backlash. Most of the young militants are still in the first flush of exhiliration over their new-found ability to tell the world what they think of it. They have not yet learned to effectively use the real political power available to them.

But I am confident that these problems are temporary, and that blacks will not waste much time in these blind alleys.

Of the three problems, the poverty problem is the most frustrating. It includes problems of the poor other than blacks: the Appalachian whites, the migrant laborers, the Mexican–Americans, the Indians. In terms of health, education, nutrition, housing, and employment, there are millions of Americans who live as no human being should have to live.

We are told we have the best medical care in the world. How, then, does one explain the World Health Organization statistics indicating that the United States ranks 24th in infant survival and 26th in male life expectancy? Certainly we have excellent medical care available to those who can afford it. Certainly many physicians devote a significant proportion of their time to treating indigent patients without charge. But this is not enough. Despite Medicare and our great public hospitals, there are millions of Americans who for economic reasons do not have modern medical care available to them. Because his mother does not have access to a doctor, a ghetto child is twice as likely to die in his first year of life as is a non-ghetto child. On the Indian reservations, the male life expectancy is forty-two—little more than half the American average.

This must be changed. Perhaps we should consider, for example, a kind of group health insurance for needy Americans, with the premiums paid in full or in part by the government. This would provide modern medical care for everyone, without lowering physicians' incomes, interfering with the patients' free choice of doctor, or introducing unwanted government control.

Similarly, American education is as good as that anywhere in the world for those who can afford it, but a child born in an urban ghetto has only a 30 per cent chance of graduating from high school, and if he graduates the odds are 1 in 2 that he will not have received what is normally considered an eighth grade education. Similar problems face many Indian–American youths.

Since World War Two our educational base has broadened enormously. Aided by tax incentives, private corporations have combined with government and colleges and universities to offer liberal scholarship and loan aid. Most brilliant youths now can go as far as their ability will take them, regardless of their parents' financial circumstances. But what of the average child, who could profit from four years of college, or at least from a good high school education? Why must he be condemned to less than a junior high school education because he was born in a ghetto, or on an Indian reservation, or to migrant-laborer parents?

The problem of education in depressed areas will not be solved easily or quickly. But clearly we must have experimentation and innovation. We must build and maintain acceptable physical plants; we must have teachers who are better trained, paid, and motivated; we must have adequate books and other supplies; and most of all, we must radically lower the student–teacher ratio. All of this requires financing; and much of this support must come from the federal government; with a few exceptions, local and state government have demonstrated they lack the resources or the will to do the job.

At the time of this writing, the country is being shocked by pictures of golden-haired Biafran children who are on the verge of death from the extreme protein-calorie deficiency condition called kwashiorkor. But here on our own Indian reservations we have children suffering from kwashiorkor! In our ghettos and our depressed rural areas, we have children who grow up on low-protein diets that are almost exclusively such foods as beans, potatoes, and gravy—a diet that frequently results in irreparable brain damage.

Our present food-stamp program is based on a sound concept, but it has serious flaws. Some communities have failed to participate at all. Also, there is the problem of families with incomes sufficiently high to make them ineligible for food stamps, but too low to afford the balanced diet their children should have. The damage to these children could be reduced by expanding our pre-school and school lunch and breakfast programs.

For one American to suffer from malnutrition is an affront to all Americans.

Low-income housing must be built by a partnership of government and private enterprise; neither can do it alone. This concept has been subject to heavy criticism on the grounds that private industry will not build low-income housing because of inadequate profit. But this could be corrected if the federal government is willing to offer sufficient tax and credit incentives.

City governments must do their part, too. The practice of inadequate garbage collection in low-income areas is shameful; any neighborhood would become an instant slum under these conditions. Similarly, the enforcement of heating and safety housing regulations in low-income areas is often lax and marked by scandalous payoffs by landlords to inspectors. Low-income areas must receive the same services and the same protection of the law as the suburbs.

Unemployment in our ghettos, Indian reservations, and depressed rural areas is far higher than that sustained by the nation as a whole during the Great Depression. However, we now have it within our power to provide useful and remunerative work for everyone who wants it. Tax and other incentives should be offered to private industry to locate in areas of high unemployment and underemployment, and to provide on-the-job training to those unable to find work. To their credit, some major corporations have already begun such programs on their own; they should be given government support and others should be encouraged to do the same.

Finally, the government should become the employer of last resort. There are polluted rivers to clean, schools and hospitals to build, ghettos to make livable and to rebuild. There is work that needs men to do it, and men who are eager to do a day's work for a day's pay. If all else fails, the government should bring the workers and the work together.

Every reasonable effort should be made, both in government work projects and by means of tax and credit incentives to private industry, to encourage the development of new job opportunities in the rural, small-town, less crowded areas of the nation. It accomplishes little to combat poverty in the urban ghetto if we do nothing to reverse the steady stream of ill-prepared people now pouring into the cities from all parts of the nation.

In general terms, I suggest that these principles be observed in attacking the poverty problem:

First, the time for action is now, not later.

Second, development of self-help abilities is far preferable to degrading and incentive-destroying charity.

Third, a combination of government and private enterprise is more likely to be effective in the long run than either acting alone.

Fourth, we must recognize that we do not know all the answers, and that we will only find them if we encourage experimentation and innovation. We must recognize that for every experiment that succeeds, there will be several that fail. We have tolerated expensive failures in military research; now we must apply some of that tolerance to the less costly but more urgent task of eliminating poverty.

If the cost of these suggested efforts is high, the cost of neglect is infinitely higher in blighted lives, mounting welfare costs, social and political unrest, and a general weakening of society. One can only guess at the price society pays for poverty and neglect; likewise, it is not possible to appraise the dividends society receives from realizing the potential of one human life.

One of the most painful paradoxes of our age has been the burgeoning surplus of foodstuffs in the United States and a few other areas of the world, and the mounting number of ill-fed people in the rest of the world. As a member of the House of Representatives, I spoke out frequently on this theme, calling for an imaginative use of our food surpluses in a "Food for Peace" development effort abroad.

In December 1960, following his election to the presidency, the late John F. Kennedy asked me to head a special new office in the White House on "Food for Peace." That office gave me a broader appreciation not only of the world's hunger, but of the relationship of that hunger to such matters as our domestic agricultural program, the need for greater emphasis on rural development abroad, and the necessity of much broader family-planning efforts. In 1964 I summarized my experiences and conclusions about these problems in a book titled War Against Want.

It was against this background that I proposed in the Senate comprehensive legislation to put the United States more in the forefront of an effort to end hunger in the world while at the same time protecting and strengthening the economy of rural America. This legislation was introduced on June 17, 1965. It was to become the basis of an Administration-backed bill, the Food for Peace Act of 1966, passed by the Congress the following year.

Much of what I recommended in a speech on the Senate floor September 23, 1965, was incorporated in this important 1966 act. The newly authorized food assistance program has not moved forward on the scale anticipated, because of the pressure on the federal budget resulting from the war in Vietnam and the preoccupation of our top officials with that conflict. Yet, there can be little doubt that the war against world hunger and undisciplined population growth is the most important war of our age.

The Most Important War

The most challenging crisis for the rest of this century will be the accelerating race between food and people. We are faced with the spectre of widespread hunger and starvation on a scale the world has never before known unless we begin today to plan for tomorrow's food needs. The nations of the earth must do more than they are now doing to meet future food demands or major starvation will be the most painful fact of life on this planet within ten years.

Even today, human hunger is a much more serious problem than is generally realized. Half a billion people suffer from inadequate quantities of food. Another billion subsist on improperly balanced diets, most notably a shortage of protein foods. Three million children die each year from diseases induced by malnutrition. Countless human beings go through life permanently crippled physically, mentally and emotionally because of inadequate protein, vitamins, and minerals in their formative years. The ever-present companions of malnutrition—lethargy, disease, and premature death —breed listless human beings who are powerless to break out of their misery and yet capable of breeding more misery for their children and for generations yet unborn. There is increasing evidence that children who are deprived of adequate nourishment during the first five years of life suffer permanent mental retardation. The brain development that is stunted from lack of protein can never be recovered.

During 1961 and 1962 when I was privileged to serve as

Speech in the United States Senate, September 23, 1965.

———

Food for Peace director for the late President Kennedy, I developed a growing conviction that the most overwhelming paradox of our time is to permit half the human race to be hungry while we struggle to cut back on surplus production and overeating. Science has broken the space barrier, but not the bonds of hunger. Today's hunger, however, is only a mild indication of the enormous food gap that looms on the horizon.

Writing in 1798, Dr. Thomas Malthus of England observed that man's capacity to reproduce his kind was so much greater than his capacity to produce food that population would soon exceed available food supplies. Starvation would then be man's lot unless his numbers were kept down by war, pestilence, or other drastic developments.

"I think I may fairly make two postulata," wrote Malthus.

"First, That food is necessary to the existence of man. Secondly, That the passion between the sexes is necessary, and will remain nearly in its present state."

As for the hope expressed by his contemporary, Mr. Godwin, that "the passion between the sexes may in time be extinguished," Malthus observed, "towards the extinction of the passion between the sexes, no progress whatsoever has hitherto been made. It appears to exist in as much force at present as it did two thousand, or four thousand years ago.

"Assuming then, my postulata as granted," Malthus continued, "I say that the power of population is indefinitely greater than the power in the earth to produce subsistence for man.

"Population, when unchecked, increases in a geometrical ratio. Subsistence increases only in an arithmetical ratio. A slight acquaintance with numbers will shew the immensity of the first power in comparison of the second."

Although it has been intellectually respectable to scoff at the predictions of Malthus in view of the unforeseen increases in food production during the past 150 years, his warnings may yet prove to be valid. Certainly, one cannot look at the projection of current food production and population growth without a sense of genuine alarm for the future. Multitudes of people are now on a collision course with starvation.

What are the facts behind this disturbing prospect?

Fact Number 1: The population of the world is now accelerating at a faster rate than is food production. It has taken the entire history of the human race from the Garden of Eden to the year 1960 to reach a global population of 3 billion people. But the most careful projection indicates that by the end of this century—thirty-five years hence—the population of the globe will be double its present size, or 6 billion. What required thousands of years to achieve will be duplicated in thirty-five years.

These figures testify to the marvels of modern medicine, sanitation, and scientific achievement in extending human life. But they also present an arresting outlook, because they are not accompanied by a proportionate increase in food production. Because food production is now lagging behind a burgeoning world population, there are more hungry people in the world today than any previous time in recorded history.

It is evident that present rates of population growth cannot continue. The most effective possible use of space and resources will not be able to keep up with human multiplication at this pace. Population growth must be slowed, hopefully by the expansion of voluntary family-planning services, which are increasingly popular in developing countries.

But the results of family planning cannot be quickly measured. For the next decade and a half, world food needs will increase radically. The babies have already been born who will need more food, and particularly more nutritious food, if they are to lead productive lives. The war against hunger must be fought urgently and won in our lives—or most of the human race will face an appalling inheritance of malnutrition, chronic illness, poverty, and famine.

Fact Number 2: The prospects for substantial increases in food production in the areas of greatest need, most notably Asia and Latin America, are not encouraging. In three regions of the world—the United States and Canada; western Europe; and Australia—New Zealand, plus parts of Argentina and southeast Asia—there are adequate food supplies. These regions have utilized modern technology, an educated rural population, concerned government, economic incentives and fertilizer, pesticides, hybrid seed, and other innovations to increase the productivity of the land faster than their population growth.

But the combined population of these food surplus regions includes only one-fifth of the world's people. The other four-fifths live in Asia, Latin America, Africa, and the middle East. These areas are increasing their populations faster than either the supply of arable land or the productivity of their presently cultivated acreage. There is today only .4 of an acre of cropland per person in Asia, as compared to 1.2 acres per person in the United States and Canada—a ratio three times more favorable for North America than for Asia.

This imbalance between people and arable land is greatly complicated by two other factors. First, underdeveloped regions such as Asia (with the exception of Japan) have not significantly increased the productivity of their cultivated acreage. Primitive farming methods, improper irrigation techniques, the lack of an educated rural population, inadequate credit and land ownership structures, ineffective political leadership, the absence of rural extension services, a shortage of capital, the lack of farm-to-market roads or a cash market for produce, and the generally low priority that many countries have attached to rural development—all of these deficiencies have held agriculture in a primitive state characterized by static productivity in most parts of the world. Secondly, population growth rates are the greatest in the regions that have the least favorable food productivity. In the 1930s Latin America exported more grain than any other region of the world, including North America. Today, three decades later, Latin America imports much more grain than it exports. Its per capita production of grain is down 16 per cent from the 1930s level. Yet, before another three decades have passed, the exploding population of Latin America will increase two and a half times. By the year 2000, nearly 600 million Latin Americans will compete for the resources that now inadequately feed 250 million. Much the same situation prevails in Asia.

Given the combination of inadequate arable land, low agricultural productivity, and swift population growth of the underdeveloped areas, the prospect for adequate diets is not encouraging.* Consider the problem of India. This nation of 450 million inhabitants is now subsisting on a nearly static local production supplemented by 3 or 4 million tons a year in Food for Peace shipments from the United States. Yet, within the next fifteen years India's population will increase by an amount equal to the present population of the United States. There will be 637 million Indians in 1980 claiming the strained resources that now inadequately feed 450 million. Highlighting recent findings of U.S. Department of Agriculture expert Dr. Lester Brown, the editors of *U. S. News & World Report* write:

> In Asia, merely to maintain present meager diets, yields per acre must increase by more than 50 per cent between now and 1980. An increase of this magnitude amounts to more than 240 million tons of grain. It would require application of 24 million tons of fertilizer a year to get such yields. In the entire world today, total production of fertilizer is only 28.6 million tons a year.

Fact Number 3: Food reserves in the United States and other food surplus countries are not so large as commonly believed. Even if the United States could find some quick and effective method of utilizing our food surpluses abroad, they would be quickly swallowed in the deepening sea of human need around the globe; so much public attention has been focused on the problem of U.S. farm surpluses that few people are aware that the surpluses are all but gone. Government acreage controls, cropland retirement, increased exports, including an expanded Food for Peace effort, have

---

* There has been encouraging progress in 1967 and 1968 in the use of new strains of wheat and rice, which have produced greatly increased yield in some parts of Asia. Mexican wheat, developed by scientists of the Rockefeller Foundation, has been introduced and is increasingly used in Turkey, Pakistan, and India. "Miracle rice," IR-8, developed at the Ford- and Rockefeller-financed International Rice Research Institute in the Philippines, has tripled and quadrupled yields. But lack of fertilizer, farm-to-market roads, storage facilities, transportation, and fully developed marketing systems—gaps that cannot be filled overnight—make it difficult to use the new varieties as widely and effectively as they must be used.

worked down surplus stocks in recent years to a level little above that needed for our own national reserves. Dried milk, a high protein food essential to school lunch and other child feeding programs, is in such short supply that our Food for Peace officials have curtailed the programs abroad of voluntary agencies such as CARE, Church World Service, Catholic Relief Services, and Lutheran World Relief.

Wheat stocks, which constitute the main body of the U.S. Food for Peace Program, have been worked down from 1.4 billion bushels in 1960 to 800 million bushels today. Corn and other feed grain supplies have been sharply reduced. Indeed, the composite wheat and feed grain reserve of the United States would scarcely meet our own consumption needs for six months if a catastrophe should wipe out our crops in a single growing year.

Recently, President Johnson suggested that the Congress consider setting aside a national strategic food reserve. If we were to carry out this suggestion and establish food reserves sufficient for six months' consumption, we would have to end our Food for Peace Program immediately or launch much greater production.

If we were to distribute our present food stocks evenly to the needy multitudes of the world, they would be exhausted in a few weeks' time. We have been shipping approximately 3 million tons of wheat each year to India—which is a sizable flow, but one must remember that India consumes 80 million tons of grain yearly and she will need twice that amount in another three decades. Even if we could supply the entire world with food (which we cannot), there would be difficulties to overcome—including the necessity of protecting the farm markets of the local producers and the markets of other exporters. Furthermore, in underdeveloped countries we are confronted with limited port facilities, inadequate storage, a lack of roads, and other problems of distribution. It is not an easy task to distribute food effectively, even when a well-meaning government wants to give it away.

In spite of the magnitude of the problem, there is no escaping the challenge of world hunger. Neither our national security nor our moral and political position in the world will permit us to turn our backs on this most important problem of the last third of the twentieth century. Furthermore, in spite of difficulties, a nation that can send a man to the moon can unlock the doors to food production and distribution.

Eighty per cent of the people of the globe live in rural areas. The majority of them are still scratching a subsistence from the soil with methods little changed in thousands of years. These are the multitudes that provided the seedbed for the sweeping communist revolutions that seized Russia and China after the First World War. Marx thought that communism would come as the logical next step after the advanced stages of capitalism. Instead, it came to the primitive peasant societies of China and Russia, while largely losing its appeal to the industrialized, urban areas of the western world.

Guided by these historical developments rather than by Marxist ideology, the ambitious leaders of China are now calling—not for the industrial workers of the world to unite, but for a long-term struggle of rural people against the urbanized western world. It is significant that the French were driven out of Indochina—not because they lost the cities, but because they lost their support in the countryside. The same situation has plagued U.S. efforts to stabilize South Vietnam for the past decade. Likewise, Castro came to power through the hills and back country of Cuba even while the Batista government held a seemingly firm grip on the urban centers.

The great contest of our time now turns on whether we or the communists can develop the most acceptable and effective pattern for meeting the hunger and misery of the uncommitted rural world. I firmly believe that we have the capacity to win that contest and in the process to improve our relations even with those peoples who have fallen under the sway of communism in Russia, China, and elsewhere.

I believe that we ought to declare an all-out war against hunger for the balance of this century. We should call on our farmers and our agricultural technicians to enlist for the duration in the war against want. We should announce to the world now that we have an unused food-producing capacity, which we are willing and anxious to use to its fullest potential. Our government should leave no doubt that we will bend every effort to see that no nation—friend or foe—starves while we permit land and surpluses to remain idle.

Communist China has called for a "people's war" in Asia, Africa, and Latin America, to win the world over to communism. But Red China has failed on the agricultural front, and the situation has been worsened by drought and other natural hazards. She cannot win a "people's war" against the developed world if we will place the welfare of people above short-term goals of military maneuvering and cold war strategy. So let us take the lead in a "people's war" with corn instead of cannon, with farmers instead of marines, with agricultural technology instead of battle plans, with food instead of fear.

The attack on world hunger must move on two fronts. First is the short-term effort over the next ten or fifteen years to make more effective use and distribution of our farm abundance abroad. This will require not only stepping up our production at home, which is the easy part of the task; it will require more technical guidance to the receiving countries in building up their port unloading and handling facilities, their storage structures and the entire system of food distribution. I believe that we can profitably double our existing Food for Peace Program within less than ten years if we will preface this build-up with improved distribution facilities abroad. It is imperative, of course, that if we increase domestic production for the attack on hunger, we use the increase for its intended purpose and not allow it to accumulate and depress our farm economy.

It must be recognized that deliberately producing farm commodities for use overseas would be a departure from past policy. Present Food for Peace efforts are based largely on the distribution of surpluses that have accumulated in spite of farm program efforts to prevent them. It must also be recognized that in most cases it is preferable, if not essential, for the developing countries to supply most of their own food needs. But the fact remains that for the foreseeable future, the people of Asia, Latin America and elsewhere cannot increase their production fast enough to meet their needs without food shipments from the United States and other surplus food areas. I cannot believe that the American people would want to leave good cropland idle at public expense while they watched hunger spread across the world.

The second and more fundamental front in the war against hunger is the urgent need for a rapid acceleration of food production abroad. We and other advanced states must assist the developing world to undertake the kind of agricultural revolution that we have experienced in the last hundred years. There is an urgent need for the knowledge and skills of our agricultural technicians, research scientists, extension workers and experienced farmers. An American Farmers Corps consisting of retired farmers or working farmers willing to take leave of their own farms for a time could perform an invaluable service abroad. There is great need, too, for more fertilizer, pesticides, irrigation development, hybrid seed, and feed-mixing equipment. Enlightened land ownership and tax policies and low-cost credit are essential to rural development. So is an improved system of rural education.

This type of aid is not inexpensive, nor is it easy to implement. But food and agricultural assistance are less expensive than military hardware, and they are much more constructive and helpful to the peoples we assist. As one watches our two impoverished friends, India and Pakistan, shooting at each other with American arms, it is difficult to avoid the conclusion that both countries need our food and our farm know-how more than they need our guns.

Much of the tension and unrest that open the way for communist inroads and violent upheavals have roots in hunger and misery. Food abundance, on the other hand, is a powerful instrument capable of replacing despair with hope and converting the seeds of violence into the foundations of peace.

Aside from the political and moral gains that would come from a broad-scale attack on world hunger, the economic benefits to the American economy would be great. We are now spending over $2 billion a year to reimburse farmers for

retiring cropland and reducing production. Through strenuous, expensive programs, we have managed to take 50 million
acres of farmland out of production. If we began now to
divert a portion of the farm control budget into the purchase,
shipment, and distribution of farm commodities abroad, we
could double our Food for Peace effort with little increase in
overall expenditures. The impact on the American economy
would be much better than our present cropland retirement
programs. Idle farms and idle acres and idle farm labor mean
a loss of income to every farm community. On the other
hand, full farm production leads to the purchase of more
farm machinery, more gasoline and tires, more trucks and
automobiles, more seed, fertilizer, lime and equipment of all
kinds. Thirty million tons of additional business for the
merchant shipping industry would be generated by a doubled
Food for Peace Program.

I have supported acreage controls combined with price
supports because such programs are essential until we develop
greatly improved distribution methods to utilize our abundance abroad. It will doubtless continue to be necessary to
have a farm price stabilization program, given the unorgan-
ized pattern of American farm producers. But large-scale
cropland retirement is not a viable permanent farm policy
for the United States in a hungry world.

Furthermore, the strengthening of the diets and the agricultural economy of the developing countries—far from removing them as potential American markets—would open the
way for new long-range markets for the U.S. Those nations
with advancing agricultural and industrial productivity are
also our best commercial customers. Canada, with a tiny fraction of the population of India, is a larger American customer
than India. After we assisted postwar Japan to develop its
agricultural and industrial economy, she became the largest
purchaser of American farm produce.

To accomplish the objectives of a ten-year war against
want, I introduced on June 17 the International Food and
Nutrition Act. That measure would authorize the expenditure of half a billion dollars the first year to: (1) purchase

needed nutritious foods in U.S. markets for use overseas; (2) increase the capacity of the developing countries to receive and distribute such food aid efficiently; and (3) strengthen the food-producing capacity of farm people in the developing world. The bill would authorize a half-billion-dollar increase for these purposes each year for seven years, to a maximum of $3.5 billion.

The bill would authorize the President to create an International Food and Nutrition Office, perhaps an expanded role of the existing Food for Peace Office, to administer the proposed program. Also, the legislation authorizes an expanding role for the United States in the United Nations Food and Agriculture Organization Freedom from Hunger Campaign and its related experimental World Food Program. As director of Food for Peace and U.S. delegate to the Food and Agriculture Conference in Rome in April 1961, I was permitted to make the initial U.S. offer that led to the establishment of the $100 million three-year World Food Program. The cooperating nations are hoping to continue and expand this multilateral food-assistance program when it is reviewed later this year. Certainly, it is to our advantage and to the advantage of those we seek to assist, to coordinate our food aid within the family of nations and with full respect for the interests of other concerned countries.

The respected editor of the conservative *Farm Journal* put the case cogently for fuller use of our agricultural abundance to feed the hungry when he wrote in the October, 1965, issue:

> There will doubtless be times when we will wonder whether anybody could help such people, or should try. But we'll have to try, and keep trying. We're spending decades—and $20 billion—to put a man on the moon. It seems at least as important to help the human race eat.

Then editor Carroll P. Streeter added:

> With half the world hungry now, and sure to be a lot hungrier before long, we haven't a moment to lose. We must comprehend this frightening prospect and think about what we will do, both with regard to our own farm plant and our program of helping the hungry world.

In a brilliant new book, *The United Nations at Work,* a noted authority on development problems, Joseph M. Jones, described the worldwide effort to drive hunger from the face of the planet as "the most hopeful enterprise of our time." To enlist in that enterprise is to enlist on the side of health, and hope, and life for mankind. It is, indeed, the most hopeful enterprise, and the most important war of our time.

Foreign Policy and
the Crisis Mentality

In his *Crisis* papers of the American Revolution, Thomas Paine observed: " 'Tis surprising to see how rapidly a panic will sometimes run through a country."

Yet Paine was so fearful of the tendency of men to become indifferent or weary in times of crisis and conflict that he believed even panics produce "as much good as hurt."

If he were permitted to review our own time, he would doubtless conclude that the problem of maintaining a proper course between panic and complacency has taken on new dimensions, for the thirteen colonies that leveled their muskets against the established order have evolved into the world's mightiest power in a highly dangerous nuclear age. This is a responsibility that demands a rare capacity to distinguish between fundamental forces at work around the globe and localized crises of uncertain significance.

But there is a disturbing American tendency to overreact to certain ideological and military factors while overlooking issues of vastly greater relevance to our safety and well-being. A civil insurrection in Santo Domingo or Vietnam is dramatic, but what is its significance compared with such quiet challenges as the proliferation of nuclear weapons, the surging of nationalism and social upheavals in the developing world, or the mounting crisis of hunger and population? What, too, is the relationship of the quality and strength of our own society to our position in the world? How will the world see us if we succeed in pacifying Vietnam but fail to pacify Chicago?

Many Americans, having grown impatient with the frustrations of the cold war, see each international tension as an urgent crisis calling for a direct and decisive attack on the enemy. Moreover, there must be no halfway measures: "Either get in or get out!" Those who suggest that there may be a proper limit to American power are branded as "neo-isolationists." A preference for the peacekeeping actions of the United Nations over a free-wheeling unilateral interventionism is, for example, a sure sign of "neo-isolationism."

I believe that, in fact, we are in danger of seeing the isolationists of the 1920s and 1930s replaced by the neo-imperialists, who somehow imagine that the United States has a mandate to impose an American solution the world around. Those who see the United States in this role not only want U.S. police action in each trouble spot, but with decisive speed. The old isolationists and the new imperialists may be cut from the same cloth in that both look with disdain on the claims of the international community in contrast with the American way.

For example, the neo-imperialists' solution to the long, inconclusive struggle in Vietnam is a crushing military onslaught. They reject the outlook expressed not so long ago by General Maxwell Taylor when, as ambassador to Saigon, he said that the issue there is "very largely a political, economic, and psychological problem." They would prefer the approach of former Senator Goldwater, who said of Vietnam: "I would turn to my Joint Chiefs of Staff and say: 'Fellows, we made the decision to win. Now it's your problem.'"

In this scheme of things, the Soviet Union and Mainland China are viewed not as major world powers with which we must live, but as diabolical conspiracies that sooner or later we must face in battle. The answer to other lesser threats, such as Fidel Castro, is the U.S. Marine Corps. If a political rebellion occurs in the Dominican Republic, send in American troops and worry about such international niceties as the UN and the OAS later. The answer to the Berlin problem is simple: "Tear down the wall."

There are doubtless many explanations for the crisis outlook.

For one thing, America is a comparatively new country that has been largely separated from the turmoil of world politics for most of our history. During the nineteenth century, we relied on the British to put out the fires that flared from time to time in out-of-the-way places. We were free to concentrate on the development of our own economy and institutions. Pulled into World War One by the course of events, we swung back to an even more ardent isolationist course in the 1920s and 1930s. It is thus not surprising that faced with a vastly greater international involvement after World War Two, we have frequently overreacted to incidents that an older, more mature society would have regarded as "business as usual."

Second, many Americans have not assimilated a sense of the world's diversity, nor do we look at events from an international vantage point. The older nations of Europe, steeped in the maelstrom of continental politics and with a century or more of colonial experience in every corner of the globe, have acquired a cosmopolitan view of the world. But when a political coup is attempted against an unpopular government in the Dominican Republic, or student rioting changes government policies in Japan, or De Gaulle seeks the leadership of Europe after liquidating hopeless French ventures in Asia and Africa, or a guerrilla movement threatens to bring down a much more generously armed American-backed regime in Saigon, we are unable to equate these events with our own experience. The revolution in mass communications instantly brings such developments into our living rooms, but there has been no corresponding increase in our capacity to evaluate the swift changes of our convulsive age.

Communist Devils

A third explanation of our tendency to react strongly to events is the unique power of communism (as a general menace) and of the Soviet Union or China or Cuba or North Vietnam (as the precise devil) to challenge a variety of deeply felt American dreams and values at their core. For the democratically oriented American public, these are evil forces that deny open political discussion, religious freedom, bona fide elections, and a framework of law and legal process. For those businessmen to whom a large portion of the world represents an essential area for expansion, communism presents a dangerous challenge to capitalist ground rules. For Americans who dream of the United States' exercising a dominant role in potentially unlimited areas of world development, to whom Theodore Roosevelt, and later, Henry Luce and others, have spoken, Moscow, Peking, Havana, and Hanoi are challenges to the American Century. And finally, for that sizeable and vociferous minority whose views are premised on the assumption that conspiracies and dark alien powers sway world affairs—to whom the late Senator Joseph McCarthy was the Angel Gabriel—communist propaganda is tailor-made.

Thus, the American consensus against communism—no matter the variety—is rooted in a very real set of challenges and denials. It is not easily dismissed as "hysteria." Its deep traditional sources lead to an almost irresistible identification of any event related to communism as a crisis, a dire and fundamental threat to basic values.

Our crisis tendency has been given additional force by the nature of our political leadership and our two-party political dialogue, especially since 1950.

In the years immediately following World War Two, thanks to the leadership of men such as the late Senator Vandenberg, our foreign policy was conducted in a bipartisan manner largely free from political rancor and partisan duels. This was the period which launched the United Nations, the Marshall Plan, Point Four, and the North Atlantic Treaty Organization.

But with the triumph of communism in China in 1949, the North Korean attack of 1950, and the breaking of our nuclear monopoly by the Soviet Union, the comparative confidence and calm of postwar American foreign policy were shattered. The first strains of the postwar world were beginning to wear on the American public even before the Korean conflict.

It was these cold-war tensions that set the stage for the poisoning of American political life by the late Senator Mc-

Carthy in the early 1950s. Many government officials and politicians still find it expedient to demonstrate their "Americanism" by frequent outbursts of rhetoric directed at the communist enemy. The two political parties, having generally agreed on basic foreign policy objectives, wage a recurring battle over which party is taking the harder line against the communists.

Foreign policy, more mysterious and remote than domestic issues, is ideal grist for the political mill. The average citizen knows enough about social security to be somewhat invulnerable to loose charges against the program. But a prediction of disaster in the Caribbean based on alleged evil in high places is beyond the capacity of our citizens to evaluate.

This kind of exercise has been a major cause of the crisis mentality. Having agreed for years on basic foreign policy assumptions and especially the containment of communism, our political party leaders have found it necessary to devise other areas of combat. Each side knows that it must capitalize quickly on even inconsequential events lest the opposition do so first, with telling political results. Politicians out of power have found it expedient to interpret each international incident as a mortal danger to the republic. Politicians in power must demonstrate that they are taking swift and forceful steps to save the nation from disaster.

No doubt the late President Kennedy benefited in the 1960 presidential campaign from the fact that Castro had come to power during a Republican Administration while at the same time the Russians were moving ahead of us in the missile race. Once in power, the new President was under pressure to take a hard, activist line on Cuba. Even after the nuclear showdown of October, 1962, when the Russian missiles were withdrawn from Cuba—a sensational cold-war victory for the United States—some politicians worked overtime to keep the crisis boiling. Any step to ease tensions was quickly branded as a softening of resolve.

American domestic political considerations have probably motivated our deepening involvement in Vietnam since the 1950s as much as any other factor. The Republicans accused the Democrats of "losing" China to the communists in the 1940s; Secretary of State Dulles did not want to "lose" southeast Asia in the 1950s and see the tables reversed. Whatever else was prudent, it was safest in terms of domestic politics to take a tough, militaristic stance toward revolutionary Asian leaders while embracing the comfortable old despotisms.

Looking back on the Bay of Tonkin incidents of August, 1964, one wonders if a crisis was manufactured by the Administration to justify a politically popular aerial reprisal against Hanoi backed by a strongly worded congressional resolution—all of this at the beginning of a national election when Administration firmness was being questioned by the political challenger.

Again in February, 1965, American planes began bombing in both North and South Vietnam in response to a night-time Vietcong attack that killed several Americans in one of our barracks near Pleiku. Senator Goldwater had earned a "trigger-happy" label in 1964 for recommending the use of American bombers in Vietnam, but Administration spokesmen rationalized the bombing in 1965 by dramatic references to the Vietcong's dastardly "sneak attack"—implying that enemy troops should attack only in broad daylight after a fair warning. Apparently our spokesmen had forgotten our pride in George Washington's "sneak attack" on the British after he and his rebel forces stole across the Delaware River.

An American Illusion

The meagerness of genuine discussion about fundamental issues and our tendency to magnify minor incidents have caused us to miss many opportunities for constructive new initiatives both at home and abroad. We have, for example, concentrated too heavily and too long on an all-out military response to the international challenge while neglecting the economic, political, and moral sources of our strength. Frequently we have confused means with ends and then argued about those means with all the passion ordinarily reserved for sacred principles. The crisis mentality and the emphasis on means always call for more and bigger weapons. The crisis addict becomes impatient when it is suggested that a nation's strength is measured as much by the quality of its schools, the health of its citizens, the vigor of its economy, and the treatment of minorities as by the size of its weapons. He lacks the perspective to realize that the steady, peaceful development of Asia, Africa, and Latin America is of far greater significance to American security than the political color of future regimes in Vietnam or in the Dominican Republic.

Foreign aid for underdeveloped countries is a favorite target of crisis-oriented citizens and legislators, who are much more comfortable appropriating $50 billion annually for arms than $2 billion for economic development. The results of foreign aid are too slow to satisfy the mind dominated by a sense of crisis. Indeed, even an economic boycott (Cuba) or limited military action (Korea and Vietnam) is frustrating and unsatisfying to the crisis-prone individual, who would prefer to "clean up the mess" overnight.

Foreign aid bills have been presented to Congress year after year as a stopgap against the spread of communism rather than as an investment in social and economic development. Poverty-stricken countries have been encouraged by shipment of American arms to build military machines as part of "the free world" defense against communist aggression. But in the summer of 1965, Pakistan threw its American-supplied Patton tanks into war with India's American-supplied Sherman tanks. The final irony came when the Soviet Union, theoretically a potential target of the tanks, mediated an end to the war. This was scarcely a convincing demonstration of U.S. wisdom in determining other countries' needs.

While recognizing our responsibility to influence world affairs in the direction of peaceful development as best we can, we will do well to heed D. W. Brogan's warning of "the illusion of American omnipotence." There is a tendency for some Americans to assume that every distressing situation, no matter how remote, is the result of a failure on our part. During the late 1940s and early 1950s, we talked about "losing China," as though we had somehow been in command of China's destiny. But as Professor Brogan has reminded us, "A great many things happen in the world regardless of whether the American people wish them or not." For example, we ought to take every reasonable step to ensure the success of the Alliance for Progress and the defeat of Castroism in Latin America, but we must also recognize that the success of these efforts depends more on decisions that are made in Latin American capitals than in Washington.

Furthermore, we must be willing to look at our own view of the world with at least as critical an eye as we apply to the views of others. Those who have suggested that college students protesting our Vietnam policy should be automatically drafted are, in effect, calling for a moratorium on conscience and freedom. It would be ironic indeed to surrender liberty in America in the name of its advancement in Vietnam. Instead of intimidating the public dissenter, we ought to welcome his independence and give his views a careful hearing. Instead of promoting the government official who plays it safe by avoiding thoughts that might irritate his superiors, we ought to encourage intellectual integrity and moral courage as the most precious qualities of the public servant.

If we are to strengthen our position in the world, we must be willing to look carefully and critically at all foreign policy assumptions, including our present course in southeast Asia and our insistence that the world's largest nation be excluded from the United Nations.

We can well afford to listen thoughtfully to the views of experienced leaders abroad, including General de Gaulle, despite his peculiar faculty for irritating Washington. The French successfully and gracefully terminated self-defeating campaigns in southeast Asia and north Africa; in the process they might have gained certain insights that are worth our evaluation.

America has achieved a position of power and influence in the world that is unprecedented. We have often used that power generously and courageously, perhaps more than any other nation of our age. I have no doubt of our capacity to respond effectively to a genuine crisis that calls for vigorous and decisive action. I should like to believe that we will also develop a talent for discovering and responding rationally to the underlying forces at work in our time. But to those innumerable tensions, struggles, and incidents of the future that we neither can nor should control, I hope we will manifest a measure of Ralph Waldo Emerson's wisdom: "Let him not quit his belief that a popgun is a popgun, though the ancient and honorable of the earth affirm it to be the crack of doom."

The Higher Patriotism

As a critic since 1963 of our growing involvement in Vietnam, I have found myself pondering anew the meaning of patriotism.

I frankly confess to being one of those Americans who is stirred by the national anthem, the Lincoln and Jefferson Memorials, Arlington National Cemetery, the National Archives where the Declaration of Independence and Constitution repose, or the magnificent Rushmore Memorial in my home state. I never turn onto Pennsylvania Avenue en route to my office with the Capitol dome glistening ahead without some quickening of pride.

Yet, in recent years our nation's course in southeast Asia has filled me with regret, sadness and dismay. I have said on the Senate floor that "our deepening involvement in Vietnam represents the most tragic diplomatic and moral failure in our national experience." We are following, I said, "a policy of madness." In my mind, our Vietnam venture is based on a crude distortion of history and an incredible misunderstanding of the forces moving in southeast Asia since the Second World War.

In the battle zones of Vietnam I have observed brave young Americans fighting valiantly for a cause they accept. These courageous young men—perhaps the finest soldiers, marines, and pilots ever to go abroad—for the most part do not share my doubts about the bloody struggle to which they have been called. Many of them resent the protests lodged against our war policy by concerned Americans.

In my own state one officer direct from aerial combat over

Commencement address, Grinnell College, Grinnell, Iowa, May, 1967.

Vietnam has taken to the political hustings to blame me and two or three other senators for American casualties. Since we have resisted the policy that sent our men to Vietnam, it is difficult to comprehend the logic that would make us responsible for their deaths, but it is a fact that the resentment of this South Dakota officer is shared by supposedly sophisticated policy spokesmen who equate opposition to our Vietnam policy with a lack of responsible Americanism or patriotism.

What, then, is Americanism? Who is the true patriot?

I am certain that this question cannot be answered with a flip declaration: "My country, right or wrong." I am equally certain that America's interest is not served by empty-headed flag waving, devoid of reflection or understanding. Neither is the national interest served by draping the American flag over minor dictators abroad whose only claim to our protection is that they are willing to assail the communists who threaten to depose them.

Nor do we serve America's interest by fighting so blindly to export freedom to Asia that we sacrifice it here at home. There is no interest in southeast Asia that is great enough to justify silencing free speech and debate in America. To those who say that Hanoi misconstrues the dissent in the United States, I would answer that we cannot afford to sacrifice free speech and the honest exchange of convictions merely because the traditions of democracy are not understood by those who have never experienced them.

Vietnam has forced me, and I suspect many other Americans, to look back to the sources of our freedom—to the enduring qualities of true patriotism.

From the beginning America was to be a nation different from all others. Even as our country took shape, monarchs in Europe were joining in an alliance to crush and suppress all opposition to the existing order. We alone were seeking to establish a nation where opposition and dissent, free inquiry and public criticism, would not only be allowed but encouraged. For it was our faith that in the unending clash of ideas we could find the surest and most liberating path to the future.

In his first Inaugural Address, George Washington warned that "the preservation of the sacred fires of liberty and the destiny of the republican model of government are . . . staked on the experiment entrusted to the hands of the American people."

When he spoke the Constitution was new and untried. In those dawning days of the Republic, after the most careful work by a company of brilliant men, he did not promise that we had created a perfect democracy or a settled society. He merely offered an experiment. We were to have the courage to test new ideas and institutions, discarding those that hindered our progress, trying those that seemed to offer hope, and changing our national course as experience deepened and knowledge multiplied.

Thus, our whole history as a nation has been an experiment. It began with those who had the courage to break from all they knew and make the perilous journey to the New World. We became a nation in violent revolution against established order and authority. We grew and prospered because daring men crossed into the uncharted and terrifying West and explored the unknown ranges of science and invention.

It is this that tells us what is most important about the American nation: America is not an established or completed institution; it is not a particular piece of geology or a collection of people. It is not even a government or a Constitution. It is a process. It is a method of liberating the skill and energy of individual men so they may contribute to the freedom and well-being of our people. Therefore, the highest faithfulness to country does not lie in blindly accepting the ideas of the past or the policies of the present, but rather in the willingness to question and challenge all that we are and all we do, so we may bring the reality of America closer to the ideal.

The right to propose new ideas and challenge old ones, to express the conclusions of mind and the commands of conscience, is often spoken of as a freedom or a privilege. It is much more than this: it is the most imperative necessity. It is not simply something we allow, but something a free society demands. It is not just something we can live with; it is something we cannot live without. It is not only consistent with patriotism; it is the highest patriotism.

First, because it is the way in which we can correct our errors before they overwhelm us. It is one of the great virtues of freedom that we are not irretrievably tied to our mistakes. At times during our struggles with dictators such as Hitler and Stalin it was said that our open society was a disadvantage; that repressive and authoritarian states could conduct more effective policies because they did not have to confront public opposition. History has proven how wrong a view this is. For when a nation that prohibits dissent makes an error, it is often compelled to follow that error toward disaster. Thus, biological studies were held back for a generation in Russia because no one was allowed to challenge the officially sanctioned assumptions. The blind sway of Hitler's racism spiritually debauched a great nation. We could multiply endlessly the examples of disastrous policies that were continued by authoritarian states for years because no one was allowed to challenge or debate them.

In the United States, we have been troubled by racial prejudice and, most recently, by the explosions in our cities. These are signs of sickness and of past failures. But it is significant that these painful problems are being openly probed, argued, and discussed across America. This is the method of the open society, and it is the formula that holds the only real hope of social and political progress. Programs as diverse and constructive as the Marshall Plan, the Peace Corps, and the nuclear test ban emerged from criticism of official programs and attitudes. What some thought was our weakness has proved our greatest strength—the freedom to shine the light of reason on folly and thus to end it.

A second purpose of dissent is to improve our institutions and our policies. It was Woodrow Wilson who wrote: "Democratic institutions are never done; they are . . . always in the making." If we are to carry on this process, to correct injustice and enlarge freedom, then we stand in constant need of light from inquiring and skeptical minds. It does no good to say we will permit only those ideas that are sound and constructive, for once you decide to silence dangerous ideas, you must establish what ideas are safe—and that power is the power to destroy liberty itself.

Looking back over our history, it is remarkable how often we honor men who in their own time were viewed as dangerous dissenters. No ideas were more radical than the proclamations of our Declaration of Independence. Those who sought the abolition of slavery were assaulted and imprisoned. Abraham Lincoln was reviled and driven from his seat in Congress because he attacked the Mexican War in terms similar to those directed more recently by senators against the Vietnam war. Theodore Roosevelt was accused of undermining free enterprise because he fought the special interests who exploited the nation's resources. Franklin Roosevelt was termed a radical, and worse, because he attacked some of the injustices of our economic system; while John Kennedy encountered bitter resistance when he demanded that we revitalize our society and begin moving with new energy. All of these men were called dangerous in their own time and are honored today. We were able to listen and adopt their ideas because we relied on the judgment of the people—not the dictates of authority—to separate the useful and necessary from the truly dangerous. As Justice Holmes wrote, "when men have realized that time has upset many fighting faiths, they may come to believe . . . that the ultimate good desired is better reached by free trade in ideas."

A third purpose of debate is the intensely conservative desire to keep us faithful to our own ideals. It is tempting, in the midst of immediate dangers and difficulties, to sacrifice principles and even liberty to the necessities of the moment. Yet it is the most dangerous course of all, for great principles do not disappear in a huge and instant convulsion, but through their steady erosion by those willing to yield to the easy path of immediate gain. For example, from the very beginning we have felt it necessary, in the words of the Declaration of Independence, to pay a decent respect to the opinions of mankind. This historic principle of American policy is far more important today when we must rely on nations in every continent for our economic health and to assist in the defense of free societies. What was once an ideal has become a necessity. We have become increasingly dependent on the help of others in constructing a decent world order yet at times we act as if no other nation existed, as if we could flaunt our power and wealth against the opposition and passions of both neutrals and allies. We appear willing to forfeit support and sympathy alike in the single-minded pursuit of our own goals. No course could be more reckless or short-sighted. Those who dissent from such policies, therefore, are not attacking this nation but patriotically trying to recall it to one of the oldest of its great ideals.

A final reason for dissent is love of country. For true love of country is not merely the willing acceptance of institutions or policies. It is the love of an idea and of the process of freedom. It demands a complex, difficult, and discriminating affection. It is a willingness to seek out injustice and try to correct it. It is a desire to avoid unnecessary danger and devastation. It is the effort to create a peaceful world environment for liberty. It is the recognition of national responsibility as well as privilege, duty as well as reward. Even in our personal lives those who serve us best are not those who flatter or agree, but those who are willing to point out flaws and errors and spur us to greater achievement. What is true for individuals is also true for the nation. If conscience tells us we are following policies that damage the country, then patriotism demands we oppose those policies.

In nearly all the critical periods of our national life there have been those who wished to suppress dissent and impose conformity. Often these efforts have had a devastating effect on the lives of particular individuals who were their victims, but ultimately, we have always emerged with our liberty intact, and the country stronger because of that liberty. If, however, we ever yield to the forces of suppression, then we will find that we have stripped the country of its ability to meet the complex and rapidly shifting challenges of the modern world. It is not simply that we need a constant stream of diverse ideas and beliefs from which to choose—although we do; it is also a question of character. The English philosopher John Stuart Mill once wrote: "A state which dwarfs its men in order that they may be more docile instruments in its hands . . . will find that with small men no great thing can be done." Conviction and dedication cannot be imposed from the top. They must spring from the free choice of inquiring and passionate men. Liberty is not divisible. You cannot be free to support and not to oppose; to approve and not to criticize. And if we wish to tap the unmatched energies of the liberated mind for the work of our nation, each man must be able to seek his own path to the truth.

This is not an easy condition. It is far easier and more comfortable to accept what others tell you, to follow established policies and ways of belief. It can take greater courage to stand in opposition to the views of your neighbors or nation than to confront an enemy in combat. My courage has been more severely tested when I have spoken out against our excessive military budget or the policy in Vietnam than it was when I was flying combat missions as a bomber pilot in World War Two. Yet, this is the most necessary courage of all. For without it we would soon slip into that complacency and inaction that is the most deadly enemy of our national safety and well-being.

In recent months, some of the most sensitive, gallant young men I have been privileged to know have confided to me that while they are not religious pacifists, they are so convinced of the error of our Vietnam policy they cannot in good conscience participate in that struggle. Their alternatives are a prison sentence or escape to Canada. These are sorely troubled young men whose courage and integrity are beyond question. I find it difficult to counsel them, but I have no doubt of their devotion to America and their essential patriotism. There is a glaring gap in our draft regulations, which gives exemption to the pacifist who conscientiously objects to the principle of all wars, but denies exemption to the equally conscientious youth who cannot accept the justice of a particular war. We sent German officers to their deaths at the Nuremberg trials for failing to refuse the orders of their government in World War Two. Yet we have no exemption for the American youth who believes that his government is on a mistaken course in Vietnam.

It is sad that the obligation and concept of loyalty to country is most often invoked by those who least understand it. Loyalty is not blind acceptance of official doctrine or conformity to established ideas. It is not simply repeating the pledge to the flag or the Declaration of Independence. It is not assuming that your country is always right and others are always wrong. It is not the belief that people who think differently or act strangely are inferior. It is not even unthinking willingness to throw one's life and limb into military combat no matter what the policy involved.

True loyalty is a guiding principle and a revered tradition. It is the understanding that life is enriched by imagination and ideas and by diverse concepts from many sources. It is obedience to the highest traditions of freedom and to law. It is the realization that this country was born in revolution, nurtured in protest, and strengthened by dissent. It is the awareness that the great experiment still continues and that it must be advanced through the free play of the inquiring mind. It is the willingness of every man to follow the dictates of his own conscience to the most spacious limits of our legal and constitutional freedoms. It is, above all, the knowledge that any effort to compress America into a single formula or set of ideas, to impose conformity or enforce support, is, in itself, the most dangerous form of disloyalty, and a betrayal of the principles on which this nation rests and on which its future well-being most urgently depends.

To remain silent in the face of policies that one believes to be hurting the nation is not patriotism, but moral cowardice. Backing our soldiers in Vietnam does not mean cheering them on to their deaths in acquiescence to what one regards as a dangerously ill-conceived course. Criticism of public policy does not weaken the nation; rather, it serves to refine, correct, or strengthen our national course. If the policy is sound, it will become better understood and therefore more effective under the searchlight of honest debate; if not sound, it can best be remedied by constructive examination and frank discussion.

"To criticize one's country," said Senator Fulbright, "is to do it a service and pay it a compliment. It is a service because it may spur the country to do better than it is doing; it is a compliment because it evidences a belief that the country can do better than it is doing. 'This,' said Albert Camus in one of his *Letters to a German Friend,* 'is what separated us from you; we made demands. You were satisfied to serve the power of your nation and we dreamed of giving ours her truth.' . . ."

The New American

"America is change, and the changes have come, often enough, in convulsive spasms. This country is the vast experimental laboratory in human relations for the twentieth century; it is, in a sense, defining and creating the twentieth century for much of the world.

"This is not a 'sick society.' It is a deeply unsettled and bewildered society, and the reason is not merely the extraordinary changes in this last generation but the speed of these changes. It is the *rate* of change that is new.

"It is absurd to believe that the races of men who turned an empty, forbidding continent into the most efficient engine of production and distribution ever seen, who created the first mass democracy with essential order and essential freedom will not solve the problems of crowding, poverty, pollution and ugliness. The solutions will create new problems, after which there will be new solutions, then new problems, and so our life will go on. Time is life. Were human problems ever totally solved, change would come to a stop, and we would begin to die."

—ERIC SEVAREID
Look, July 9, 1968

A century ago, Charles Dickens began *A Tale of Two Cities* with these now familiar phrases:

It was the best of times, it was the worst of times; it was the age of wisdom, it was the age of foolishness; it was the epoch of belief, it was the epoch of incredulity; it was the season of light, it was the season of darkness; it was the spring of hope, it was the winter of despair.

We can perhaps say again of our own day that it is the best of times and the worst of times. This is a time when the proudest and most advanced cities in America decay at the center and erupt in violence. But it is also a time when our most sensitive citizens and urban leaders are exploring new paths to rebuild and redeem metropolitan America.

This is a time when rural America is caught between the rising costs of modern technology and stagnant farm commodity prices—an economic pressure that is driving 600,000 Americans annually from the farms and small towns into already overcrowded cities.

But it is also a time when American agriculture with its amazing productivity can help point the way to a world free from want and an economy marked by a prosperity and a charm that could be the envy of the most favored urbanite.

This is a time when precious lakes and streams are polluted, when the city air reeks with smog, and much of the countryside is littered and marred.

But it is also a time when Americans are beginning to think seriously about beauty and conservation, leisure and recreation, and perhaps a newer and better style of life.

This is a time of violence that has struck down John and Robert Kennedy as well as Medgar Evers and Martin Luther King.

But it is also a time that has created these great leaders and their dreams of an America moving ahead in a climate of peace and dignity.

This is a time when many youths are alienated from the political, social, and religious institutions of our day.

But it is also a time when young people are reaching out for a more honest, open idealism that may lead us into the light of a new day.

This is a time when the world is caught up in a grim, accelerating race between an exploding population and inadequate food production.

But it is also the first time in the long history of mankind that we have the technical capacity to end hunger and misery on our planet.

This is a time when racial tensions and the frustrations of the poor run high across the land.

But it is also a time when growing numbers of American political leaders and citizens have come to understand that none of us can be fully free until every American has achieved a full measure of economic and social justice.

This is a time when America is caught in the grip of the Vietnam tragedy—perhaps the most unfortunate venture ever undertaken by this nation.

But it is also a time when we may be learning painful lessons about the limitations of military power and the hazards of intervention in the affairs of turbulent nations still in search of their identity.

As one views this panorama of darkness and light, he might well recall the words of Edmund Burke two hundred years ago: "I am aware that our age is not what we all wish. But I am sure that the only means of checking its degeneracy is to concur heartily with whatever is best in our time."

One of our difficulties is that it is not always easy to know what is best in our time. Indeed, nearly all major groups and institutions in our society seem to be questioning their own values and modes of operation. No first-rate educator is really satisfied with the present organization and methods of even our most prestigious universities, or with our elementary and secondary teaching methods.

Our major churches are questioning not only their organizational and denominational patterns, but their fundamental role in society.

The leaders of the labor movement—once the most progressive and innovative of men—are now challenged both from within and outside labor's house by those who yearn for a more compassionate and perceptive leadership. The leaders of minority groups and the poor are questioning each other as to the most appropriate areas of struggle and the most fruitful techniques.

Among the leaders in agriculture, no major farm spokesman would contend that he has found the whole answer to the difficulties of rural America. In foreign affairs, we are coming to see that old assumptions, which have guided American foreign policy for a generation, are no longer appropriate for today or tomorrow.

And in my own field of politics, perhaps most of all, there is a growing recognition that the old politics must and will give way to the new. Growing numbers of people are determined to end such anachronisms as our outmoded and undemocratic procedures for nominating presidential candidates. The need for a more efficient and responsive Congress is painfully clear to all with eyes to see. But beyond these specific areas of necessary reform, there are new currents in American politics that may very well change the whole style and tone of our political life. As George B. Leonard, senior editor of *Look,* put it in a stimulating article in the May 28, 1968, issue of his magazine, "Something is stirring in American politics. There is an excitement in the air, a sense that we can find our national purpose once more—but in a new way."

I am convinced that out of all this questioning and probing and ferment, a new American is struggling to be born—an American who will draw heavily on the richness of his past but who will also reach out to the new dimensions of today's world.

I believe that new American will have, first among his characteristics, the understanding that his capacity for grace —his love and concern for his fellows—is more significant and necessary than an unbridled individualism or an intellect devoid of compassion. It is just not possible for human life to flourish on this increasingly crowded planet unless we come to understand that brotherhood is the prime condition of our survival. If we have anything worth learning from the hippies' message, it is a kind of gentle doctrine of love that is as old as Bethlehem. In its best and most practical sense, love is a force that can remove mountains of fear, and division and self-destruction.

I have often wondered, as a Protestant, why the late Pope John warmed my heart as he did the hearts of people from villages and farms and cities all over the world. It was not his intellectual power. And it was not his articulate oratory, for he lacked that capacity. I believe it was his simple compassion, his warm humor, his love for ordinary human beings. These are qualities that could well grace the new American.

The new American will also know—especially if he is a politician, a preacher, a journalist, or a teacher—the importance of speaking clearly his truest convictions. He will shun the tendency to live by public opinion polls, or popular pressures, hypocrisy or opportunism. "To thine own self be true . . ." will guide his life.

If I have learned anything worth passing on to others in fifteen years of active political life, it is the importance of saying what one really believes rather than trying to tell the other fellow what he may want to hear at the moment. I have kept silent or modified my views a time or two because I feared public reaction, but I was wrong in doing so from the standpoint of my peace of mind; furthermore, it is bad politics. The people prefer straight talk to the "credibility gap."

When I first spoke out against the Johnson Administration's policy in Vietnam, I was concerned about the political consequences, but South Dakotans welcomed it—even though they weren't sure I was right. Few of them agreed with me on this issue five years ago; today, I suspect that most of them do. At least they want me to continue saying what I really believe. Honesty is not only the best policy; it is the best politics.

As George Leonard writes: "It may even be possible for some present-day candidate to subvert one of the parties toward openness and encounter. He could start simply by being himself. Even now, anyone who cuts through the sham and scheming, who is entirely honest about his actions, motives and feelings, might well electrify the voters and become a real threat to the pros."

The new American won't duck the hard issues and fall into easy slogans. For example, as I have argued earlier, we need to face up to the present military draft and replace it with a volunteer system. Why should a free society try to get by on forced labor and cut-rate wages to provide its military defense? On a related issue, let us ask whether it makes sense for the United States to continue maintaining 300,000 American troops in western Europe twenty-three years after the end of World War Two. The prosperous nations of western Europe are capable of providing their own military manpower needs; yet because of inertia and a distorted sense of our mission in the world, we continue, at great cost to our balance of payments position, our taxpayers, and perhaps even to our international posture, to maintain these costly forces in an area where they are no longer needed.

The new American will also recognize that it is not enough to be a protester and a dissenter, or to "turn off" and "drop out." One must also be an innovator, a reformer, and a redeemer. To protest "the establishment" demands also a willingness and a capacity to build anew; it calls for some measure of grace and staying power, not a fragile or rigid withdrawal in the event of one or even many defeats.

And the new American will appreciate that American power in the world is not based primarily on armaments, but on the actual living of our spiritual and political faith. There is no more urgent imperative than to correct the excessive allocation of our resources to military hardware and ill-advised ventures abroad. American society cannot longer afford to throw two-thirds of the entire federal budget to the military. Neither can we afford to let military doctrine dominate our policy-making process.

The great lesson of Vietnam is that we cannot transport freedom and dignity or even security and peace in a B-52. There are crucial problems in this world that even the mightiest military weapons cannot reach. World peace and domestic tranquility based on justice and dignity are the great unfinished tasks of our time. They will come, not at the point of a gun, but through the compassion, the liberal spirit, and the wisdom of Jefferson and Lincoln.

The day of unilateral intervention is over; the need for more effective international peacekeeping machinery is clear. Also, the practical advantages of directing economic development assistance through multilateral channels is equally clear. No single nation has the power, the wisdom, or the mission to be the world's policeman, banker or judge. These are the functions of the United Nations, the World Bank, the World Court, and other agencies of the international community.

The Peace Corps has sent thousands of conscientious Americans to developing countries around the world. This program has benefited not only the recipient countries; it has added meaning and purpose to the lives of the volunteers and has returned to the United States a rich harvest of understanding and respect. At the same time, we have sent 500,000 brave fighting men to Vietnam—30,000 of whom have lost their lives. This costly effort has not only failed to accomplish its stated purpose of self-determination for the Vietnamese; it has killed, wounded or displaced millions of Vietnamese. It has exacerbated rather than ameliorated the problems of that country, it has alienated many of our best young people from their own country, and it has done much to destroy the moral leadership we once held around the world. What would have happened if, instead of sending 500,000 troops to Vietnam, we had sent 10,000 Peace Corpsmen armed with medical ability, agricultural know-how, sanitation and nutrition skills, and dedicated teaching talent, and had left the Vietnamese to develop their political and economic institutions in their own way?

I see two other qualities in the citizen fathered by these new times. First, the new American will understand that the unique genius of America is in the motto "E Pluribus Unum" —from the many, one. America at its best is one nation—not a nation that pits urbanite against farmer, rich against poor, white against black or red or brown, or youth against age.

And finally, the new American will recognize that it is not nearly so helpful to do things for people as it is to create the conditions in which people can do things for themselves.

I don't believe that the poor, our minority groups, or any other group of Americans, really want a dole. What they desire is a recognition of their worth as individuals and their right to an equal opportunity.

I know from countless conversations with farmers that they

do not want hand-outs. They want fair prices, reasonable interest rates, the opportunity to bargain effectively, and an end to unfair competition from tax dodgers and corporate agriculture. In the cities, people want jobs and training and education and a chance to do a day's work for a day's pay.

The nation has drifted into a serious population imbalance between rural and urban areas. During the past two decades, some 18 million Americans from the farms and small towns have left those areas and gone to the cities. They have done so, in many cases, not because they prefer the city with its overcrowding and congestion, but because of declining economic opportunities in rural areas. The result is a twofold problem of serious dimensions: (1) a loss of human resources to maintain the institutions of rural America and the small towns, and (2) an addition to the already serious problem of overcrowding in the cities.

The answer is not a dole to take care of the city's new migrants from the farm and town; nor is the answer found in a dole to keep them in rural areas. But it is clear that both urban and rural America suffer from a condition that finds 70 per cent of our population jammed into 1 per cent of the land area, with the proportion heading rapidly toward 80 per cent by 1980. Why not, then, a program of tax incentives to encourage industry to locate and provide jobs in the less-populated states? Why not incentive credits to industries that will agree to perform government contracts in the sparsely populated areas? Why not a farm program designed to provide better income incentives and credit to young men wishing to make a career in agriculture? Why not a greater effort to encourage Indian, Mexican–American, Negro, and other low-income American groups to engage in job- and educational-training programs in their own areas with tax and credit incentives to those industries that work with them?

These efforts can help correct the mounting rural–urban population imbalance, and they represent the kind of self-help initiatives that the new America requires.

I believe that the late Robert Kennedy, at the time he was struck down, was arriving at a clearer understanding of the demands upon the new American than any other leader of his generation. It was he who beckoned us in the words of Tennyson: "Come, my friends, 'tis not too late to seek a newer world."

It is not too late, but we need to be about the business of a newer America and a newer world.

ABOUT THE AUTHOR

GEORGE McGOVERN, Senator from South Dakota, was born in Avon, South Dakota, on July 19, 1922.

A professor of history and government at his alma mater, Dakota Wesleyan University, he was elected to the U.S. House of Representatives in 1956 and re-elected in 1958. He was a U.S. delegate to the NATO Parliamentarians Conference in 1958 and 1959.

McGovern was named Food for Peace Director and Special Assistant to President Kennedy in January 1961. Elected to the U.S. Senate in 1962, he is a member of the Committee on Agriculture and Forestry and the Committee on Interior and Insular Affairs, where he serves as chairman of the subcommittee on Indian Affairs.

Senator McGovern is the author of two books: *War Against Want,* published in 1964, and *Agricultural Thought in the Twentieth Century,* published in 1967, as well as articles for *Look* magazine, *Atlantic Monthly, Saturday Review, Commentary, The New Republic,* and other leading journals.

The Senator and Mrs. McGovern have four daughters and one son.